"Insightful and incisive, *The Woman in the Story* is the first road map to previously uncharted screenwriting territory. Whether devoured whole or in bite-sized pieces it never fails to engage and inform."

— Robert Jones, Producer, *Dirty Pretty Things*

"As a film producer, whose life is spent submerged in scripts; living and breathing the evolution of a character, it is wonderful that a screenwriting guide to the female character has been written with such intelligence, sensitivity, and insight by a hands-on experienced female writer."

— Suzanne Mackie, Producer, *Calendar Girls*

"Just the bi-line makes me want to write a screenplay with women in it so I can use this book!"

— Gillian Anderson, Actress/Director, *The X Files, The House of Mirth, Bleak House*

"Helen Jacey's book is an excellent resource for writers looking to create complex, compelling, and truly 'memorable heroines.' With our screens dominated by strong male characters, *The Woman in the Story* should be a catalyst for many equally exciting roles for women."

— Kate Kinninmont, CEO,
Women in Film & Television (UK)

"*The Woman in the Story* gives an in-depth approach to what goes on in the minds and hearts of female characters. It is thought provoking and informative. I especially loved Jacey's exploration of the internal wound, internal gift, external wound, and external gift. This book will help every level of writer learn to write from a place of greater consciousness and will, in turn, connect the audience to their story."

— Jen Grisanti, Story Consultant
and Independent Producer

"Helen Jacey's book, although focusing on writing women, isn't just a handbook for creating great heroines (or villainesses)... it's an easy-to-read workshop, full of lessons, techniques, and exercises to help you craft great characters of any gender."

— Chad Gervich, Writer/Producer: *Foody Call, Speeders, Reality Binge, Wipeout*; Author: *Small Screen, Big Picture: A Writer's Guide to the TV Business*

"Helen Jacey has written an insightful, utterly compelling book about female characterization that is as insightful as it is instructive. It is an essential volume for screenwriters and film students everywhere."

— Jonathan Sothcott, Producer,
Dead Cert and *Devil's Playground*

"Jacey dissects the female role in many films and applies that to the elements of bringing together a competent screenplay with female protagonists. The book makes an engrossing guide for anyone looking for insight into the female psyche and hoping to strive for something new and original instead of harping on the same doldrums we've seen in hundreds of films before."

– Felix Vasquez Jr., Cinema Crazed

"Helen Jacey has created a much needed blueprint to creating strong female characters. All screenwriters—male and female—who are interested in writing films with strong female leads should be smart and start their process by using the advice and tools in this book. I look forward to seeing the multitude of films that come from people trained by Helen Jacey in the belief that women's characters and stories are valid, valuable, interesting, and necessary."

– Melissa Silverstein, Founder,
Women & Hollywood, *www.womenandhollywood.com*

"Every now and then a book comes along that sheds a completely new light on the screenwriting process. *The Woman in the Story* is one of those books and long overdue. Taking the thorny subject of female representation, Jacey asks the questions that should be at the forefront of developing convincing and believable female characters but rarely are. Screenwriters will be reassured and stimulated by Jacey's direct and motivating approach. Teachers of screenwriting will breathe a sigh of relief that they finally have a toolkit that will help students avoid clichés and stereotypes in character development."

– Lucy Scher, Director, The Script Factory

"Once I got my hands on a brand-new copy of *The Woman in the Story*, I couldn't put it down. I was still reading it at 2 AM and can hardly wait to apply Helen Jacey's suggestions to my own screenplay, effective immediately. As a screenwriting professor, I'll be adding it to my course bibliographies. Many of my screenwriting students are going to fall in love with this book next semester!"

– Alexis Krasilovsky, Professor, Screenwriting Option,
Department of Cinema and Television Arts
California State University, Northridge;
Writer/Director, *Women Behind the Camera*

"This book delves deep and comes up with revelatory ideas about female characters. It is profoundly original, distilling and transforming the way you see women from Scarlett O'Hara to Juno. Jacey provides an inventive and wonderfully clear guide to bringing female characters to life. A brilliant resource for filmmakers working on projects that focus around women. The first book to think about screenwriting and gender—and about time too! This is a "how-to" book with a real difference."

– Sarah Gavron, Director, *Brick Lane*, *This Little Life*

HELEN JACEY

THE WOMAN IN THE STORY

WRITING MEMORABLE FEMALE CHARACTERS

Published by Michael Wiese Productions
12400 Ventura Blvd. #1111
Studio City, CA 91604
tel. 818.379.8799
fax 818.986.3408
mw@mwp.com
www.mwp.com

∾

Cover design: MWP
Book design: Gina Mansfield Design
Editor: Christine A.T. Dunn

∾

Printed by McNaughton & Gunn, Inc., Saline, Michigan
Manufactured in the United States of America

∾

Library of Congress Cataloging-in-Publication Data

Jacey, Helen
The woman in the story : creating memorable female characters /
Helen Jacey.
    p. cm. -- (Great unproduced film scripts)
    Includes filmography.
    ISBN 978-1-932907-79-7
1. Motion picture authorship. 2. Motion picture plays--Technique.
3. Women in motion pictures. 4. Characters and characteristics in
motion pictures. I. Title.
    PN1996.J26 2010
    808.2'3--dc22
                                        2010018596

Mixed Sources
Product group from well-managed
forests and other controlled sources
www.fsc.org Cert no. SW-COC-002283
FSC © 1996 Forest Stewardship Council

for Patrick

TABLE OF CONTENTS

ACKNOWLEDGMENTS

Serendipity has played a big part in the creation of this book, as so many special people appeared at exactly the right time. Most of all, I want to give special thanks to Michael Wiese, visionary publisher, for his trust, guidance, and belief. Not only was Michael astoundingly perceptive about the need for this book, but also his amazing insight helped bring it into being. Linda Seger's writing has been highly influential to me over the years, not only inspiring my own screenplays but also my exploration into women and film. I am deeply touched by her generosity in writing the foreword to this book. I would also like to thank Ken Lee at MWP for all his efforts and Christine Dunn for her thoughtful editing of this book. Thank you!

Much of this book draws on my life as a screenwriter, and all the following people have helped me in far too many ways than I can mention here: Phil Parker, great friend, mentor and teacher; my agent Elinor Burns, for endless hard work and commitment; Jenne Casarotto, for her helping hands; Nicholas Horne and Mark Casarotto, for never making anything feel like a problem; Gareth Wiley, for his belief and encouragement; Lucy Scher, for her unstinting faith and friendship; Amelia Bullmore, Lucy Floyd, Sarah Flint, Becca Mackenzie, and Emma Ko, for moral support and friendship over the years; Margaret Glover, for being the right person at the right time, and Michael Lutin, for saying the right thing at the right time; Briony Hanson at the Script Factory for her dynamic energy; Kate Kinninmont at Women in Film and TV UK for her warm enthusiasm and support. I would also like to thank all the many women and men participants who have come to my seminars and workshops, for sharing their own experiences of writing heroines with me and making training so enjoyable. I would also like to acknowledge and say a big "thanks" to all the producers who I've worked with over the years and have helped me learn "on the job." This book wouldn't exist without you.

This book really came to life at Anne and Lawrence Hansen's wonderful home in France. I cannot thank them enough for all the love, practical support, encouragement, and delicious meals!

Every daughter needs a mother who teaches her how to question, and I was blessed that I didn't have to look too far for mine. For her boundless generosity and rare gift of understanding, I am indebted to my mother Anne, true friend and unsung heroine. For telling the first stories, I'd like to thank to my father John.

For endless encouragement and support in their own unique ways, I would like to thank my family, particularly Stephen, Anna, Claire, Ant, Rachael, Mark, Alex, Billy, the two Sonias, Elliot, Abigail, Suzanne, and Michel. Loving gratitude must go to Jack, who continues to teach me everything about motherhood and how to stay on the sunny side of the street.

FOREWORD

Every era has issues to confront that affect the arts, politics, economics, relationships, and the drama of our time. Many films and characters reflect, comment on, reveal insights, and shine a light on our world, whether it's the multiple themes of World War II (*Schindler's List, Inglourious Basterds, Holocaust, The Pacific, Letters from Iwo Jima, The Diary of Anne Frank*) or about corruption (*Wall Street, State of Play, Blood Diamond, The International*) or the complexities of the Vietnam War (*Platoon, Apocalypse Now, Casualties of War*) or films revolving around women's changing roles and identity (*9 to 5, Working Girl, My Brilliant Career.*)

During the last fifty years, almost every aspect of society has been affected, in one way or another, by the Women's Movement. Yet characters in film have been slow to reflect the many dimensions of the changing identity of women. Characters in modern film usually have more shading than the stereotypical dumb blonde or the aggressive female boss, but large chunks of female dimensionality are still missing.

This may be a result of few guides to lead us. Or because writers are so busy expressing their art and learning their craft that they have little time to think of the nuances that shape characters. It's easier to write a general female character that looks like everyone else, and hope that Julia Roberts or Meryl Streep or Sandra Bullock will bring the character to life, than to write the needed extra dimensions to the role. But the truth is, an actress won't, and can't, express complexity if it's not on the page. They can't make up what isn't there, in spite of their considerable talent and skills.

We still struggle with what makes a great character of any gender, and with what makes a great female character. We continue to ask: "Is she just like a man, but she looks different?" Or is there something different operating because of her different physicality and different social influences? If so, what does she look like? Act like? What are the challenges, obstacles, and metaphors that govern her psychology and behavior? And how do you express these nuances without sounding like a psychology book or a feminist rant?

That's why we need books like this. Film is one of the most persuasive and influential art forms, and most writers know this. Most writers don't just write on a lark, but they write to tell us something about our lives. They bring characters to life and these characters move us, touch us, lead us, guide us, and, when done well, tell us something about who we've been, who we are, and where we're going. When writers accept that they are doing more than self-expression or trying to make money or gain fame, many writers will admit they're driven by the desire to bring meaning and contribute something worthwhile, perhaps even to change the world as we know it.

Writing is said by some to be a "sacred trust," and many of the best writers recognize that writers have a responsibility, not only to their characters and their subject matter, but to be a light to society.

To do this, they need to know the world and its inhabitants. They need to be in tune with the forces of the times. They need to be able to create, shape, and detail character flaws, insecurities, and know why they're there. They need to know the context in order to create characters in context. It's admirable work.

I always hesitate to tell anyone "you must read this book." You have free will to choose any book that seems to fit your need to know and that pulls you to be a better writer. But I'm so tempted to use those words like "must" and "should" and "have to" with this book, because this book is not just good and helpful, it's important.

Writers illuminate the human condition, and the more one understands the human condition, the better the possibility of shedding some light on the issues, possibilities, and challenges of being human and bringing these meanings to life through characters.

It is our generation, our era, that has done much exploration of what it means to be female. It's not feasible to have a great female character without some understanding of where she fits in the overall scheme of things. Yes, there are thousands of books you can read to understand women from the viewpoint of psychology, sociology, education, economics, and myth. But there are very few books to help you understand females from a cinematic viewpoint. Helen Jacey has written a guide, an encouragement, an illumination to light the writer along the way.

Dr. Linda Seger
Author of *When Women Call the Shots, Creating Unforgettable Characters, And the Best Screenplay Goes to…*

INTRODUCTION

I must admit, deciding to write a screenwriting guide about half of the human race has felt strange at times. Don't screenwriting principles apply equally to all characters? Aren't conflict, character arc, theme, and structure, universally true *because* they apply to every type of hero, male or female?

It was Linda Seger, writing *When Women Call the Shots* (1996) who first made me realize that all the dramatic theories from Aristotle have been written by men, and that it's time for new models for stories about women. But none of the screenwriting guides have paid much attention to the differences between men's and women's lives and to what happens if the hero is a heroine. None of them have seriously worked out what happens to the rules and conventions if a heroine leads the action. If you want to write a screenplay with a female character, there's a good chance some of your questions won't be easily answered.

As a screenwriter, I had the same recurring dilemmas every time I began a story with a female main character. Certain questions would float around my mind, along these lines:

- Why do I think a heroine might make my story work better?

- Why am I writing her like this?

- These scenes don't need conflict. Something else is going on.

- Is she a stereotype? Is this clichéd?

- She isn't returning to her old life. She's moving on forever!

- Why does she have to be younger?

- Too unlikeable? I've seen plenty of dark male heroes be or do that!

- I know a female audience would get her, but how can I convince any one else?

It isn't just me. I have met many writers who ask similar questions and have similar thoughts about feminine identity; the reality of growing up as a female; female biology; whether any of these "eternal" truths of drama actually change when a female character leads the story; and our fears of unwittingly recreating a stereotype or softening a character to make her "more sympathetic." So I sat down and worked out some of the answers for myself.

The Woman in the Story is the result of many years of literally "thinking heroine," to work out why some female characters are truly unforgettable and others just fade away with time. This book is the conclusion of a long, eventful, and often emotional journey inward to my own creative consciousness and outward to the real-world demands of the film industry. I have read, thought, discussed, and debated the subject of heroines with friends, family, filmmakers, producers, directors, agents, screenwriting gurus, and countless numbers of filmmaking students. I have watched hundreds of films from all over the world.

I will share with you a set of principles that have made the most sense to me when it comes to creating great females character. Even if your heroine was first created in a novel by somebody else or was a true-life person and the subject of biographies, and even if it will be an actress who eventually gives your character flesh and blood, it is your job, the screenwriter, to make sure she has the best chance of survival by making her as *memorable* as possible. *The Woman in the Story* aims to help you do this.

The Woman in the Story asks you to take risks and think flexibly. The principles will introduce you to new ideas, stimulate your thinking, and might even validate what you intuitively know to be true as a writer. You won't find the words *universal* or *eternal* here, because when it comes to female characterization, so much has been, and will remain, in flux. There's no right or wrong way. I am sure that as stories with heroines evolve, so will these principles.

I sincerely wish *The Woman in the Story* helps you create a memorable heroine.

Helen Jacey

THE POWER OF THE HEROINE

Chapter 1

WHY CHOOSE A HEROINE?

Before we get started, sit back and take a long hard think about why you want to choose a heroine as the main character in the first place. Hopefully, at the most basic level you want to further the cause of womanhood with your story, and obviously you want a woman's point of view. Some of your reasons might echo any of these motivations:

- To show a real woman's life (biopic). That includes my own!

- To show a woman getting over betrayal/trauma and finding a new life.

- It's about a love affair.

- It's about relationships.

- It's about a woman finding out what she really wants out of love and life.

- It's a rite of passage, as a girl becomes a woman.

- To show a mother/daughter or a mother/son relationship.

- To show the conflicts between motherhood and career.

- It's about a group of nuns in a convent in eighteenth-century Spain.

- To show the struggles of the female artist.

◌◌ My heroine's a survivor, and I want to show her struggle to empower herself.

◌◌ I want her to be strong, without giving up her femininity.

◌◌ It's a chick flick about finding love and lots of shopping!

◌◌ It's about a group of female friends who....

◌◌ To show a lesbian relationship.

◌◌ It's about an older woman who....

◌◌ She's a female android who....

◌◌ It's sci-fi about a matriarchal society.

◌◌ None of these. My main character just happens to be a woman. It makes no difference what sex my character is.

Do any of these feel familiar? If so, it is no surprise because most of them are motivated by one underlying creative urge — to explore a woman coping with a situation and how that situation is affected *because* she is a woman.

Both women and men are given femininity and masculinity as roles at birth. Our gender is like an invisible gift from our parents and our culture, regardless of what we choose to do with it later as adults, like transsexual Bree in *Transamerica*. The same goes for your heroine. Whoever she is, and wherever she is from, your heroine will reflect what you want to say about femininity, whether you are saying this consciously or unconsciously. You will define her character, choices, and journey according to these decisions.

Whether you think men and women are born different or made different by culture, your story will reveal your own personal "take" on masculinity and femininity. To borrow from one of the late Blake Snyder's principles, your take on gender is an "immutable law of screenplay physics."

For those of you who believe we are all equal now, or that men and women have the power to live anyway they choose, or that even in certain areas women are overtaking men, there's no getting away from the fact that thousands of years of one sex's domination over another has lingering side effects that don't wash easily away in a matter of decades. You might put the differences between men and women's lives down to evolution or culture, but the truth is, even if the gap is getting closer, women's real power is recent. The heroine you write, and her story, will inevitably reflect what you truly believe about the difference between men and women. Even if you think no difference exists. Your conscious and unconscious attitudes about women and femininity, once your film is made (and assuming your heroine hasn't been fundamentally changed during the filmmaking process) will be out there for all to see. Film is a very powerful medium. It influences, challenges, distorts, and reflects aspects of human life. So it is a good idea to be fully conscious about the heroine you are creating and what she represents. *So write exactly what you want to represent in your heroine.* Let's take a look at a couple of examples, *Aliens* and *Chloe*, to see what they could be saying about femininity.

The Talented Ms. Ripley in *Aliens*

Aliens could work equally well with a male protagonist, and as a sci-fi, it's not about "women's lives." The heroine Ripley is single, has no (surviving) children, and is devoted to her career. She doesn't look overtly feminine in her image, and she is as assertive as the best of the guys. Well, as strong a woman as Ripley is, her impulse to care and protect the little girl Newt is not equaled by any of the others on board. As the film progresses, we are gripped by watching Ripley deal with the maternal role in so "alien" an environment. Having lost her own child, she's getting another chance at motherhood by caring for Newt. Isn't *Aliens* really saying that all women, even strong types like Ripley, are endowed with the maternal instinct no matter how many guns they wield? Isn't it showing the battle of all battles between over-protective mothers? Could the film be seen as suggesting that women are the natural carers of children *because* of biology?

Certainly Ripley was a herald to a new era in terms of representation of strong women. The theme of maternal instinct in an action/thriller/sci-fi was exciting. But take a peek beneath the surface, and you find a "take" on femininity because it is *an immutable law of*

3

screenplay physics. Now let's look at the more contemporary *Chloe* to see how the writer shows femininity.

Return of the Vamp in *Chloe*

Chloe follows Catherine, a middle-aged gynecologist, whose paranoid fantasies about her husband's lack of fidelity lead her to un-ravel. She ends up having steamy lesbian sex with a sociopath prostitute. By the end of the story, things are so out of hand that Catherine has to save her family from a destructive hell of her own making. Some women relate to the themes that *Chloe* explores, such as the fear of being unattractive to your husband, who is maturing while you are "aging" and the fantasy of making love to another woman. Catherine's dilemma also reflects a certain truth in that many men and women do not want to destroy the family unit because of a reckless and impulsive sexual desire. *Chloe* gives the female audience a fantasy and a morality tale in one.

But no woman could call *Chloe* a "progressive" film. It's offensive to lesbians by incarnating the centuries' old psychotic and insatiable female predator stereotype into a young female prostitute. The story hints loudly that prostitution in women is dysfunctional whereas it's okay for men if they keep it quiet. The male characters are innocent and trusting; their happiness is in jeopardy because their insecure wife and mother isn't coming to terms with aging very well. Catherine's husband doesn't even mind she's had sex with a woman when she finally confesses. There isn't much in the story that asks the audience to think about sexual double standards. If anything, *Chloe* is telling the female audience that no one said life is fair!

MASCULINITY AND MALE HEROES

Male heroes also give the audience a perspective on masculinity. The writer might be doing it consciously or unconsciously, because he or she thinks they are just telling a story. Men's lives, conquests, journeys, achievements, interests and concerns, fears and desires, are rarely labelled as "masculine" but that's exactly what they are. Battles for territory, from Wild West epics to mafia supremacy sagas, to even more personal stories of a man's personal struggle or need to find love show the filmmakers' take on masculinity as much as any film with a woman in the lead reveals a take on femininity. More often than not, the women characters in the hero's story will be products of the writer's take on women and femininity.

It's time to pin yourself down. What is your motivation and personal take on things? What is your story with a heroine going to say about women and their feminine roles? Whatever your own slant, it will affect your characterization, story, and themes. If you aren't sure, let me help you think more about it by introducing you to something I call the Feminine Superthemes.

THE FEMININE SUPERTHEMES

I like to think of the Superthemes as the deepest, most underlying core beliefs behind our desire to choose a heroine. Having written and watched many heroine-led films, I've come up with what I believe are the four main Feminine Superthemes in movies with female leads. Now every time I write or watch a movie, I can't help but categorize it according to these Superthemes. I also call them the four Fs.

- ∞ Familiar Femininity
- ∞ Feel Good Femininity
- ∞ Fighting Femininity
- ∞ Future Femininity

A Feminine Supertheme reflects your conscious and unconscious attitudes about women and gender and shapes all your narrative choices.

If you're like me, and you write with a great deal of female main characters, you will soon see certain ideas re-emerging with each project. Sometimes it feels that you are covering old ground, even if you've chosen a distinctly different heroine, setting, plot, theme, and even the genre. It's as if a certain *sensibility* or an *ideological slant* infuses your work. If you haven't been writing for long, then you might get a familiar reaction to movies with heroines. Some films might profoundly move you, as if they resonate deeply. Other films might totally get your back up and leave you feeling angry and dissatisfied with the moral or thematic implications of the film, even if there's nothing you can really put your finger on.

Think of a Feminine Supertheme as if you are wearing tinted shades when you write your heroine's story. You see her and her world through a colored tint or tone, which reflects your own conscious and unconscious attitudes toward women. These instinctive responses boil down to the human need to see a true reflection of our core beliefs, which have been created by our personal experience and understanding of life. By getting to know the Superthemes you can see which influence you and your writing most. Remember, like all the principles in this book, they aren't rigidly defined categories. These are aids to help you reflect on the wider context of your story. In this respect, several Superthemes might function in your story. It's just that often one tends to dominate. That's because our stories will always reflect our personal attitudes and beliefs.

A Supertheme is not the same as the genre of your screenplay. Nor is it a "controlling idea" or theme of your narrative. It is not the same as the topic, central idea, or underlying message of truth you are exploring. For example, *North Country* is a drama about a woman fighting for her rights to be a miner without denigrating sexual harassment. *North Country's* theme is the pursuit of justice. The film's "issue" is women working in male-dominated industries. None of these are *North Country's* Supertheme, which co-incidentally is Fighting Femininity, as you'll soon see why! So now let's find out more about the Superthemes, and see which ones you relate to most.

SUPERTHEME 1: FAMILIAR FEMININITY

If you're a Familiar Femininity writer, you have a strong motivation to create a heroine who isn't out to change the world. To you, feminism has righted some wrongs and given women equal status, but it isn't really necessary any more. You might think that feminism wants everyone to be the same, and deep down, you don't think that's right. Your heroine isn't going to question her identity as a woman, and neither does her story. She could be a wife or a mother, or well on her way to being one, as she's a family maker at heart. When you write with Familiar Femininity as your slant, it's a bit like you are telling yourself, "*I'm not out to change the world, just saying it how it is.*" You like functional relationships, happy families, and stories with a heart of gold. Most of all, you want to tell a good story, with empathetic leading characters.

You might want to celebrate everyday women in their ordinary lives. You will be a writer who has a strong affection for relatively uncomplicated women. Not too complex, ball breaking, or dark. Rocking the boat is not your style. You're not out to change the world with your heroine, you don't want her to suffer too much — and if she does, you make sure she survives, usually with the help and loving support of a good man, her family, or her good friends. Familiar Femininity films show women trying to find a husband, getting married, being wives, being good mothers, or being innocent victims who end up being saved by others. The family unit is important to your heroine and is even central to her identity. She is a functional human being, whose solid values might be rocked from time to time but remain intact. If these women suffer, often it's because they've been betrayed. They aren't having trouble dating, getting divorced, or having midlife crises. They might be in trouble and need help. The heroine in *Slumdog Millionaire* is a product of Familiar Femininity Supertheme. She is beautiful, nice, loving, and loyal, and only stops being a victim because the hero proves he is a worthy and stable mate. *Army Wives* and *Brothers and Sisters* are both shows with the Familiar Femininity Supertheme behind it too.

These heroines aren't women who actively question expectations upon them as women. They would prefer not to fight the system because they want to believe in it. Rooting out corruption and lack of morality can often be a feature of their stories. *The Good Wife* is basically Familiar Femininity, but it has a dollop of Fighting Femininity, in that the heroine is definitely questioning her values after her husband's betrayal. Even if life is hard for your heroine at times, she ends up with her value system firmly intact, if a little shaken. *Chloe* is a great example of Familiar Femininity as we have just seen, in which the family stays together, and the destructive seductress dies (after a remarkable lack of characterization). A truly memorable heroine of the

Familiar Femininity Supertheme is Nanny McPhee in *Nanny McPhee*. Highly unattractive by conventional standards, which might be the reason for her single status, she facilitates happiness and well-being in families.

When you look at some Familiar Femininity box-office hits, you can see the appeal to the wide audience. With Familiar Femininity your audience is mainstream. In *Marley and Me*, Jennifer gives up her career to become a mother, support her husband, and be there for the children. The marriage relationship almost crumbles under a ton of stress by the reality of bringing up young children, giving up dreams, and losing a great deal of sleep. But you never once feel that she is going to turn around and leave. She is stressed out, but she isn't wrestling with her choices on a deep level. If anything, it is husband John who has the life-choice dilemma when he compares himself to his achieving, freedom-loving bachelor friend.

Familiar Femininity is the Supertheme behind many period romances. It's alive and kicking behind most Jane Austen adaptations, for instance. The heroine might be clever and quirky, she might be embarrassed by the overt femininity of superficial female relatives, but at the end of the day, happy marriage, after being bailed out by a man, saves the day. How many versions of *Pride and Prejudice* do we need to get the point that Elizabeth Bennett ultimately needs Darcy to sort her life out? The answer: a lot! The mainstream audience never gets tired of this happy ending. Likewise, in *The Young Victoria* Queen Victoria wants to serve her people well but her own inexperience, isolation, and need to prove herself create hell of her own making in the form of political and marital crises. She has turned her back on Albert, her husband. Order is restored by Victoria coming to her senses and realizing she will be a happier and wiser monarch if she shares her power with Albert. Another British monarch, Elizabeth II, in *The Queen* is more attune to the trauma suffered by her own family, when her daughter-in-law Diana, Princess of Wales, dies, than the needs of the British people. It takes the patient dedication of Tony Blair to help Elizabeth remember her duty in a time of crisis.

SUPERTHEME 2: FEEL GOOD FEMININITY

Feel Good Femininity is the driving motivation behind films with heroines who want to live life on their terms as empowered women. As a Feel Good Femininity writer, you want your heroine to indulge in all that is relationship-orientated, from sex to marriage to children to multitasking. You probably believe feminism has truly empowered women, and that women are now able to redefine femininity for themselves in every area of their lives: motherhood, image, purchasing power, sexuality, relationships, and work. Sure, men might have it easier, but women have great lives and things are getting better all the time. You might prefer to call yourself postfeminist rather than feminist, which sounds too angry. You probably are deeply fascinated by the emotional journeys of empowered heroines, in particular how contemporary women deal with relationships with men (and sometimes women, in the case of *The L Word*, the L.A.-based lesbian TV show).

Your heroine might be looking for love, but she's doing it with open and curious eyes. She's nobody's victim but her own. If a guy hurts her, she generally ends up working out that she was partly to blame. In *He's Just Not That Into You* Gigi goes from being a woman who will do anything to get a boyfriend only to realize her low self-esteem is more damaging to her than any male rejection. If your heroine has got issues with men, she will engage in the battle of the sexes with zest while learning her own lessons along the way. She might have emotional wounds, but she will heal them in order to find the right soul mate or to move on happily single. Some of the most famous heroines to emerge out of this value system in recent years are Carrie, Samantha, Charlotte, and Miranda from the TV show *Sex and the City*, and a growing audience has followed their trials and tribulations as women getting older. *Sex and the City: The Movie* showed a more serious side to love and the difficulty of true communication.

You could say that Feel Good Femininity gets a kick out of women obsessing about being women. These films show ultrafeminine, often affluent, worlds where fashion, glamour, shopping, cooking, beauty, and motherhood are pleasurable pastimes that are presented as central to female identity. This is why films infused with the Feel

Good Femininity Supertheme get quite a great deal of stick for being too conventional and not going far enough to challenge stereotypical notions of women. Their critics accuse them of being too conventional despite all the vibrators, sex wars, and relationship obsession.

I believe the widespread appeal of these films for women (and they do well at the box office) is that they can contain a great deal of emotional truth at the same time as they celebrate the more enjoyable aspects of women's lives. *The Holiday* is a great example of two women coming to terms with their emotional wounds, which are getting in the way of having good relationships. These stories can laugh at what's great and what sucks about being a woman in equal measure. They have resolutely happy endings, often with the heroine finding Mr. Right, but most people, men and women, do want to find their soul mate. These stories reflect this shared romantic wish back to the audience.

Male characters in these films are never out and out bad guys, oppressing the heroine. If they are negative, they reflect the heroine's own inner problems. Big and Carrie's relationship in *Sex and the City* (show and movie) is a great example of a male and female character both healing their respective emotional wounds to be able to love. Very often the story reveals the bad boys are only bad because of their own psychological baggage. Daniel in *Bridget Jones's Diary* knows he's a compulsive womanizer and laughs at his faults, which is all part of his seductive charm.

Feel Good Femininity films are the female equivalent to the male action-adventure. Call it gender escapism. These films take their rightful place alongside comfort food and shopping binges. When it comes to mainstream movies, many men crave the adrenalin and suspense of heightened masculinity, and women enjoy the emotional satisfaction and fun of heightened femininity. This is a generalization, but the box office figures back it up. Romantic comedies and what I call dramatic comedies (see Chapter 8) abound, *Confessions of a Shopaholic*, *The Holiday*, *Something's Gotta Give*, *Legally Blonde*, *Baby Mama*, the list is endless. Feel Good Femininity also alive and kicking in TV with *Desperate Housewives*, *Gilmore Girls*, *Mistresses*, *No Angels*, and *Weeds* to name a few. These films and TV shows can and do take a poke at the establishment. At the end of *The Devil Wears Prada* Andrea shuns the shallow world of fashion, but it has taught her some valuable lessons. Like it or not, Feel Good Femininity is here to stay!

SUPERTHEME 3: FIGHTING FEMININITY

Fighting Femininity is exactly how it sounds: Your heroine has a major problem with the worse sides of sexism and the "patriarchy." *Patriarchy* is a seriously unfashionable term (a bit like *feminist*), but it's useful to describe the system that a Fighting Femininity heroine meets head on. If you are interested in heroines embarking on "women against the system" journeys, this is the Supertheme for you. As a Fighting Femininity writer, you're motivated by women, who, despite victimization and oppression, find it within themselves to get up and fight despite the odds. You like writing about heroines who take on the boys and win. Or if they don't win, and your heroine has a tragic ending, there's no doubt what is to blame — the patriarchy!

You're a writer who *knows* that power structures have been limiting women's lives for millennia, and you are motivated to write a story to show it's still going on. You might not call yourself a feminist, but your narrative gives you away! One thing is for sure, you think there are still changes that need to be made, and you might even believe something of a backlash is going on against feminism. If you had a song as your theme tune, it would be *I Will Survive*. Even in the domestic sphere, you want to see your heroine breaking out of limiting confines to be free. Nazneen in *Brick Lane* escapes the dominance of her husband by gaining confidence in making her own decisions and finally emancipating herself and her daughters from his repressive expectations. Heroines like Shirley Valentine (*Shirley Valentine*) and Thelma and Louise (*Thelma and Louise*) all share a need to break out of domestic drudgery.

Sometimes heroines empower themselves, against all odds. Erin Brockovich (*Erin Brockovich*) is an impoverished and uneducated single mom. She takes on a corporate giant and wins. Through thick-skinned determination and economic desperation, she singlehandedly changes her own life, those of her children, and a community. In *Rabbit-Proof Fence*, three little 'half-caste' aboriginal girls evade institutionalization at the hands of a cruel man in order to search for their natural mothers.

If you like to write biopics about women, you have a great range of Fighting Femininity films to inspire you. Historical films, such as *The Duchess* and *The Other Boleyn Girl*, show heroines whose lives are crushed by male domination. In *The Hours*, the pain of being a woman in a highly restrictive world is sensitively explored through interweaving story lines, in which three very different heroines, one of whom is Virginia Woolf, make painful choices in an attempt to live life on their terms. Similarly, *Sylvia* shows the plight of a sensitive female genius Sylvia Plath when she marries egocentric womanizer Ted Hughes. Her ability to write is compromised by the stress of isolated motherhood and her emotional torment over Ted's affairs. In *Frida*, fragile physicality and a roving husband are both obstacles to, and fuel for, Frida Kahlo's art. Fighting Femininity stories don't all have to be doom and gloom. *Bend It Like Beckham* gives a humorous take on traditional Sikh values getting in the way of a teenage female football fanatic's dreams. *An Education* tells a true and humorous coming of age story about Jenny whose affair with an older man nearly jeopardizes her chance of going to Oxford. During her story, Jenny tries to make sense of the limited lives of the women around her, leading her to finally make a choice that helps her truly grow.

Many films with heroines from world cinema reflect Fighting Femininity, reminding us that many women's lives in different parts of the world are still unequal. In *4 Months, 3 Weeks and 2 Days*, in which the heroine Otilia has to support her friend through the harrowing ordeal of an illegal abortion, women's powerlessness and sexual double standards are explored in-depth. *Maria Full of Grace* shows a young Mexican woman oppressed by a sexist Latino culture where opportunities for women are so grim she would prefer to risk her life and that of her unborn child by becoming a drug mule. The plight of Indian women is brought carefully home by Deepa Metha's films, *Fire, Earth,* and *Water. Curse of the Golden Flower* follows an Empress in dynastic China trying to escape the emotional and physical tyranny of her husband, who finally accepts that her husband's power is unbeatable and she will only find freedom through death. Contemporary French cinema is on a roll in making films influenced by Fighting Femininity, but with a dark twist. The work of Catherine Breillat

(*Romance*, *A Ma Soeur!*, and *The Last Mistress*) gives us heroines who have no bounds exploring their feminine fantasies.

Men in these films tend to reflect sexism and misogyny on either personal or cultural levels. They can be cruel control freaks or powerless good guys. Sometimes the heroine has to challenge a woman or group of women who are upholders of a sexist system. The heroines of *Mona Lisa Smile* and *The Devil Wears Prada* all take on a dominating woman or women who represent backward attitudes toward women. In Tarantino's *Kill Bill Vol. 1* and *Kill Bill Vol. 2*, "The Bride" empowers herself to exact deadly revenge against both her male and female persecutors.

Even comedies reveal the Fighting Femininity Supertheme, such as *St. Trinian's*, in which the anarchic femininity of school girls rules the day as they take on the government inspectors to save their school. *The Stepford Wives* and *Down with Love* also critique the damaging restrictions of gender roles by using parody.

SUPERTHEME 4: FUTURE FEMININITY

The Supertheme of Future Femininity fuels the motivation of writers who want to write a good story in which the hero just happens to be a woman. You are a Future Femininity writer if you really want to avoid explorations of femininity. You aspire to write stories that reflect true equality in a world where gender conflicts have been solved, and women don't feel the need to reclaim femininity, obsess over it, or fight it. It's not that you're uncomfortable with it, you simply want to write a story with a strong female character. You feel the future is here already, and you don't want to get bogged down in agonizing about gender issues. You might even identify with the approach of a male director who told me (on writing female characters) "I write them as men and then given them female names." With Future Femininity, your take on femininity is as a by-product of your story and not a driving concern that motivates you. Future Femininity is a vulnerable Supertheme because when you have a heroine, it can be difficult to avoid "being a woman" issues as they take over and infuse the story. It can happen intuitively, as you rewrite draft after draft, or because others in the development process want you to make your story more about women's issues or your heroine's sense of femininity.

Rendition is a good example of Future Femininity. Reese Witherspoon's main problem is to find out the truth about her husband and to get him home safely. The fact that she's a mother is not the main issue. Nor is she feeling oppressed because of her gender, because it is the decisions of a powerful woman that have led to her husband's incarceration. She's angry because her husband has gone and everyone is lying! The Coen brothers' movies tend to reflect Future Femininity, not by ignoring gender roles, but by revealing the dark and ugly sides of masculinity and femininity that men and women use to their advantage to gain power over one another. *Burn After Reading* and *Intolerable Cruelty* reveal this cynical take on gender.

When you are motivated by Future Femininity you can make a conscious decision to subvert gender roles, so that traditional expectations of male and female characters are minimized. Male characters can be nurturing and empathetic without anyone making a big deal out of it. Female characters might have a great deal of power over men in the story. All of this is coincidental. A heroine might be the breadwinner, with a supportive male partner, and it just isn't an issue.

As you probably guessed, sci-fi and utopian films are great contenders to write with the Future Femininity Supertheme. By removing the female character from the reality of the world as we know it, you can automatically liberate her characterization from real-world expectations. Buffy in *Buffy the Vampire Slayer* is a good example of a woman not beset by gender concerns, who leads a team with nice guys. *Star Trek*, *The Matrix*, and *Avatar* all give us female characters (not heroines, mind you) who have an external problem that is paramount to the plot, and any questions or issues about femininity are secondary.

Television is full of shows with Future Femininity at work, particularly in thriller and crime stories. *CSI: Crime Scene Investigation*, *Prime Suspect*, and *Damages* are shows in which the heroine has a clearly external problem and being a woman is not the main deal. With investigative thrillers, these heroines are focused on solving crime. You can keep the gender exploration in the background, although it will still come through. For instance, *Prime Suspect* has a distinctly Fighting Femininity undercurrent.

You can use biopic as a good genre for Future Femininity films if your heroine's life is defined by a passion. For instance, *Silkwood* and *Gorillas in the Mist* are good examples of women with driving passions in their careers, and in which the external problem and goal are not overshadowed by questions or explorations about femininity. Likewise, *La Vie en Rose* is a brilliant example of character-driven study of Edith Piaf that follows her rise as a singer and her battle with self-destructive addictions because of the poverty and emotional abuse in her childhood. Singing is Edith's survival strategy and source of life. It is true that all these films reflect Fighting Femininity to a certain extent, as these heroines get where they want to be by snubbing conventional expectations to pursue their dreams. By focusing on what your heroine is actually passionate about, your story can dilute the impact of the other Superthemes.

So these are the four main Superthemes. There is actually a fifth, Fantasy Femininity, but it's one where memorable heroines do not thrive, in fact it produces the opposite: unmemorable stereotypes of women. Fantasy Femininity is behind the films and genres in which female characterization remains two dimensional. Slasher, horror, and action films are the main perpetuators. The audience tends to be young and male. This isn't to say that some writers try to subvert the stereotypes in certain genres (think *Jennifer's Body* and the more recent James Bond films like *Quantum of Solace*), but escaping the fantasy element is difficult. Why fantasy? Because the characters are either idealized male fantasies of femininity or projections of misogyny, and most women just can't relate to them. Women are young and beautiful, either victims or betrayers, and exist to be saved or brutalized by men.

EXERCISE: SCREENWRITER'S SELF-ASSESSMENT QUESTIONNAIRE

Okay, now it's time to think about you, the writer. Have a go at filling in the Self-Assessment Questionnaire, the first of many that appear throughout this book. Most of them are going to be addressed to your heroine, but sometimes they'll be addressed to you.

Even if you do not have a writing project at the moment, still try to complete it. It's amazing what you can find out about yourself when you give yourself the time. You might even get an idea for a new heroine's story!

SCREENWRITER'S SELF-ASSESSMENT QUESTIONNAIRE

1. Why do you want to write this story?

2. Which audience is your story aimed at?

3. If you could choose five adjectives to describe the situation of women in your culture, what would they be?

4. What are your five favorite films with heroines? Why?

5. Do any of the Feminine Superthemes feel more relevant to the female-led films being produced in your own culture?

6. If any film with a heroine particularly annoys you, can you say why?

7. If you have a project started, do you think any of the Superthemes are influencing you? How?

8. If the story you want to write could be described as a cross between two known films or shows, what are they?

THE MEMORABILITY FACTOR

Now that you've worked out which of the Feminine Superthemes could be motivating your desire to create a heroine, it is time to think about who she is going to be. Why her? What's so special about her? Why does she appeal to you? How is she going to appeal to your audience?

There is a good chance that you may already know who your heroine is. She might be based on a true-life story and a thinly disguised version of you! She might be someone completely fictional, invented by your originality. Alternatively, she might be a fusion of all these things, influenced by who you are, the women you know, other screen heroines, and your own wild imagination.

Whoever she is, your aim is to create a heroine who will launch thousands of viewers to their screens and will keep them there, gripped and entertained. They want to see a memorable character telling a story that might be true to life, but that is portrayed in a unique way.

CHARACTER VERSUS STORY

If a fantastic story idea or a high concept is your driving inspiration, then you will be creating a heroine to lead that particular idea afterward. It is inevitable that her characterization will be "story" or "plot" led. What do I mean by this?

Well, a high-concept pitch is one sentence that sets up the central problem or situation of a character and gives it an ironic twist. Most high-concept heroine-led films tend to come out of the U.S. and can be comedies, romantic comedies, thrillers, or supernatural films; all the solid genre fare. Comedies, ranging from *Overboard*, *Bringing Up Baby*, and *Roman Holiday* to the more recent *Bride Wars*, *Legally Blonde*, *What Happens in Vegas*, *Just Married*, and *The Proposal*, all promote certain predictability in the main problem of the central character, which you can sum up in a one-line pitch. In a comedy, we know the heroine or heroines are usually going to resolve their problems, we just want to watch how they pull it off. We also want to see a memorable heroine who makes the inevitable fun to watch. If it's Sandra Bullock serving up a tried-and-tested romantic comedy formula by doing a goddess dance around a fire, then fabulous! We know where we stand.

Ideally, you will find a strong story and create a memorable heroine to lead it. Take for example the following premise: "A female poet is on the verge of suicide when her estranged mother asks her to move in and take care of her." Here, the poet is undefined, but she faces a tricky dilemma. Her already miserable life made even more so by caring for an elderly woman who could be responsible for her problems in the first place. Or is she getting a new chance to heal old mother/daughter scars and start again? In this situation, your job would be to develop a character that can make the unfolding dilemma as richly complex as possible.

With the ever-increasing number of heroine-led films, we're moving into an era in which the character and her situation are gaining supremacy over the concept. Take *The Holiday* and *The Break-Up*. In both films, there is no central irony or dilemma that has to be worked out; the heroine's own self *is* the main problem. We want to watch the heroine dealing with her personal issues that sabotage her happiness. If there's any irony in the story it arises out of a conflict between what she thinks she wants and her actual emotional capacity to get it, over and above her external dilemma. In *The Holiday*, Iris thinks she wants Jasper. By switching houses with Amanda, a stranger she meets on a home-exchange site, she embarks on a process that will transform all her feelings about herself and her expectations of love. In *The Break-Up*, Brooke's desire to make Gary miss her brings about an ugly separation. She eventually understands neither of them was ready for a committed relationship for totally different reasons.

In both films, the story concept *is* compelling. There's a fish-out-of-water aspect to *The Holiday* as both women swap houses, and a "how not to save a relationship" irony to *The Break-Up*. But I think that in both movies, the complexity of the characters has the edge.

CHOOSING A CHARACTER

As we all have to start somewhere, I suggest you choose a heroine now, begin developing her, and then move on to work out her story. I hope that by the time you've got to the last page of this book, your character and your story will have gone through a huge number of changes. You will have fresh insights, new inspirations, and, hopefully, bigger and better ideas. That's the whole point of rewriting and development, and reading books like this one! So don't fret if you have a tendency to be commitment-phobic with your characters when beginning a new story idea. Your heroine will grow on the job or fail spectacularly.

If you've written many stories with heroines, you probably know that all your characters go through monumental transformations each time you rewrite scenes, sequences, or full drafts. A heroine can change her voice and her attitude from scene to scene. On a bad day, it can seem you are subjecting your character to a series of brain transplants or in a worse-case scenario, a frontal lobotomy. When your screenplay goes into a development process that has to take into account the creative input of others, the number of surgeons and diagnoses only increases.

EXERCISE: FINDING YOUR HEROINE

So why her? Why this strange female creature lurking in your subconscious? I'm sure there are many others suitable for the job of leading your screenplay, so what is it about this one?

Let her tell you. She's got to fill out the Application Questionnaire for the Role of Heroine. The purpose of this exercise is to bring your heroine into existence. She's not carved in stone, and you may yet trade her in for a different model. During the remainder of this book, you will get lots of chances to develop her characterization. See yourself as her coach on the job!

APPLICATION QUESTIONNAIRE FOR THE ROLE OF HEROINE

1. What is your name? Any nicknames? How do you feel about your name?

2. Why do you want to lead this screenplay?

3. What do you feel you can bring to the role?

4. Why would audiences like you? For your strengths or your weaknesses? Why might they dislike you? What's your dark side?

5. Give me three reasons why I should give this job to you and not to anyone else.

6. What are your personal goals and objectives for the future? Do you expect to achieve any of these during this screenplay?

7. Are you married, single, or divorced? If married or single, are you happy about that? If divorced, what went wrong? Are any issues from your past relationship going to get in the way?

8. Do you have children? If yes, do they live with you? Do you expect them to accompany you in this story? What childcare needs will you have?

9. Where do you live? Describe your neighborhood. Why do you live there? Are you planning to travel or relocate in the course of the screenplay?

10. Tell me why you think an audience would remember you.

11. What are your notable achievements? Might the audience have already heard of you? Are you famous, or celebrated?

12. Finally, if you were a flower, what flower would you be? Why?

How was that? I hope you found a suitable candidate! For those of you who already know who your heroine is, I recommend you still complete a few "application forms" on behalf of other potential competing candidates in the waiting room of your mind. Sometimes the favorite doesn't win the race.

THE MEMORABILITY FACTOR

So what's going to make your heroine and her story stick out? Let me introduce you to a fun but highly important concept: the M-Factor.

Your heroine's M-Factor (shorthand for Memorability Factor) is the incredibly unique and unforgettable quality that has never been seen before. In the highly competitive industries of film and TV, and with all the proliferating new media platforms available, you have no choice but to make your heroine uniquely distinctive. The M-Factor will:

- Inspire your writing of the screenplay, causing you to jump out of bed each morning and race to the laptop.

- Make her stand out to script readers, who can only recommend her to the powers that be.

- Intrigue producers and make them sleep uncomfortably at night if they reject her or make them excited to be giving her a shot.

- Make an actress want to bring her to life.

- Make her reach wide audiences who will never forget her!

But wait a minute, you might be thinking. How can I know this when she's only just got the job? You can't. Not fully, because what a director and actress bring to your heroine's M-Factor are vital to the process. But as the screenwriter, you get first shot. So the sooner you find her M-Factor, the sooner your writing will be reaping the rewards.

Despised, Admired, and Memorable

To find the M-Factor of your heroine, first step back a little. Brainstorm some heroines you know and place them under the following categories:

∽ The most despised
∽ The most admired
∽ The most memorable

It's a fun exercise and better to do in a group. What you will come away with is a series of extremely passionate comments about which famous heroine falls into which category. Try not to fall out!

Here are some of mine:

Despised: Annie Wilkes (*Misery*), Scarlett O'Hara (*Gone with the Wind*), May (*The Mother*), Joan Crawford (*Mommie Dearest*), and Vivian Ward (*Pretty Woman*)

Admired: Scarlett O'Hara (*Gone with the Wind*), Deloris Van Cartier (*Sister Act*), Maria (*Maria Full of Grace*), Otilia (*4 Months, 3 Weeks, and 2 Days*), Precious (*Precious*), Elizabeth (*Elizabeth*), Elle (*Legally Blonde*), Ripley (*Alien Trilogy*), Jackie Brown (*Jackie Brown*), Clarice Starling (*The Silence of the Lambs*), Nazneen (*Brick Lane*), and Grace Augustine (*Avatar*)

Memorable: Scarlett O'Hara (*Gone with the Wind*), Dora (*Central Station*), Precious (*Precious*), Erin Brockovich (*Erin Brockovich*), Bridget Jones (*Bridget Jones's Diary*), Ada (*The Piano*), Fausta (*The Milk of Sorrow*), Edith Piaf (*La Vie en Rose*), Lee Holloway (*Secretary*), Jane Tennison (*Prime Suspect*), Thelma and Louise (*Thelma and Louise*), Julia Child (*Julie and Julia*), Nanny McPhee (*Nanny McPhee*), Celie (*The Colour Purple*), and Marie Elena (*Vicky Cristina Barcelona*)

As for my "despised" heroines, there aren't too many. If anything, the majority of the ones I've listed are the main antagonist in the story, not the lead role. This is because of the strong tendency to make heroines very sympathetic. Compulsive heroes like those of *Citizen Kane* to *There Will Be Blood* are rarely women, as I'll talk about later in the chapter "Unsung Heroines." And why is Vivian in *Pretty Woman* here? "Despised" is probably too strong a category, but in my opinion, she is essentially a "fantasy" heroine... a too beautiful "tart with a heart" who finds a super-rich soul mate. She just isn't real!

Scarlett O'Hara from *Gone with the Wind*, with all her petulance, self-seeking, feistiness, determination, and positivity comes into all my categories. She would make a nightmare sister, a worse friend, and, as she says herself, a terrible mother. If I had to choose one of her qualities or vices that stood out, it has to be her selfishness. Scarlett O'Hara makes a mockery of the term *dramatic arc*. She goes through lots of changes, more external than internal, but her fighting (selfish) spirit is never crushed. This is her admirable quality and key to her survival. Selfishness makes her determined and indomitable, from the beginning to the end of a three-hour movie.

With your "memorable" group of heroines, now find the one dominant quality that really stands out. This is probably her M-Factor, or pretty close to it. You might need to brainstorm around all her other character traits. Here are some of my suggestions as to why some famous heroines are memorable:

- Bridget Jones: blundering neurosis
- Precious: survival against the odds
- Erin Brockovich: gutsy tenacity
- Lee Holloway: contented masochism
- Amanda Woods: high octane vulnerability
- Vera Drake: misguided generosity
- Julia Child: bubbling positivity
- Jane Tennison: gritty loner
- Nanny McPhee: stern healer
- Marie Elena: unboundaried passion

And some lesser-known heroines from world cinema:

- Maria (*Maria Full of Grace*): determined risk taker
- Fausta (*The Milk of Sorrow*): acutely fearful
- Anais (*A Ma Soeur!*): dark for her young years

It can be a great idea to rent out films from much earlier decades, like *Gone with the Wind*. Actresses like Irene Dunn, Mae West, Lana Turner, Greta Garbo, Bette Davis, Doris Day, and Marilyn Monroe frequently played heroines with the M-Factor. But these stories were created in eras before feminism, and their stories can reflect limitations in women's lives in those eras. Being "spunky" or a "femme fatale" was often the only personal agency these women had!

It's really simple. Your character's M-Factor is her defining and standout quality. You could call it her essential self. It's the reason why she will be memorable.

The M-Factor Equation

Here's a really simple equation to find your heroine's M-Factor. Treat it like poetic math!

M-Factor = [your heroine's compulsive need
+ most shocking/difficult trait] × charismatic or endearing quality

Let's put it to the test with one of my favorites, Dora from *Central Station*. Dora's work as a letter writer for the illiterate (whom she calls "trash") is jolted when the mother of Josue, a nine-year-old boy, is killed. Dora reluctantly agrees to help Josue find the father he has never met. Let's find her M-Factor. First, I would say Dora's most compulsive need is being a loner and baggage-free. Her most shocking/difficult action or trait is deceiving her clients by not sending their letters after being paid for writing them. Her charismatic quality is her sharp tongue.

Dora's M-Factor = [loner *(compulsive need)*
+ unremorseful deception of clients *(irreverent action)*]
× sharp tongue *(charismatic trait)*

Dora's M-Factor = tricky old grouch! Dora is the dramatic and female equivalent of Carl in the animated movie *Up*. They share a very similar story, as old people on a quest with young children in tow. Dora, as an older heroine, is notable for her age and sex alone, but the fact that she's unpleasant and clearly wounded makes her all the more fascinating. Remember, when it comes to writing heroines, *whoever dares wins*. The writers created a truly memorable heroine in Dora, and the movie and its creators went on to win countless awards.

Let's try one more with Scarlett O'Hara, as she's so outrageous and another personal favorite.

$$\text{Scarlett's M-Factor} = [\text{self-seeking } (\textit{compulsive need})$$
$$+ \text{ outrageous manipulation } (\textit{shocking trait})]$$
$$\times \text{ optimistic determination } (\textit{charismatic trait})$$

Scarlett's M-Factor = ruthless prima donna! The success of *Gone with the Wind* is legendary. Like her or hate her, nobody forgets Scarlett O'Hara.

Likeability

One thing that jumps out is that the M-Factor has nothing to do with how sympathetic or how "likeable" your heroine is. This is not the place to worry about alienating the audience. She needs to be *complex* but not necessarily *nice*. Think about all the complex, dark, male heroes that have entertained and compelled millions to watch them in recent years. The more complicated, wounded, and alienated the better when it comes to men, it seems. The perennial problem for writers is fear the audience won't like the heroine. Making the main character likeable is an issue for all writers, but it is more of a tricky issue when it comes to heroines. We're encouraged either to generate huge levels of sympathy for a heroine in order to justify any difficult choices she might make or to make her as sympathetic as possible. It is very hard for writers to avoid this pressure.

I'm going to talk more about this in the chapter "Unsung Heroines," but in the meantime remember that a million heroines die the death of oversoftening every day of the year. They drown in the *sea of forgettability* because they simply aren't complex enough. This doesn't mean that your character has to be tricky, just as long as she isn't too bland. Your M-Factor has to have the X-factor, basically.

Remember Scarlett.

In Search of an M-Factor

An example of a heroine in need of an M-Factor is Fanny Braun in *Bright Star*. It is a beautiful film, depicting a sensitive and feminine exploration of love, but sadly Fanny is not particularly memorable. Why? In my opinion, Fanny's characterization falls between too many stools; she isn't nice enough, passionate enough, or dark enough. To be nicer, she should have been written to show warmth and care about her lover Keats. To be darker, she could have been written as a seductive waverer, the commitment-phobic female who isn't going to let an ailing and impoverished poet change her life. To be more passionate, she could have been written as tossing her heart to the wind and not letting anything stand in her way of being with Keats. She wouldn't have let him rot in a squalid London room all alone when he's fighting tuberculosis. She would have put up a real fight to go to Italy. *Bright Star* is a true and tragic love story that reflects the stifling limitations and entrapment of women, but it is one of those films in which the male love interest, the sensitive Keats, possibly has more of an M-Factor than the heroine.

A MEMORABLE STORY

Once you have found you heroine's M-Factor, you will eventually have to create a story that illuminates it brilliantly. An effective way is to put your heroine in a situation in which her M-Factor is sorely tested. By putting her under pressure, your heroine will learn which aspects of her personality help her and which aspects hold her back. Remember the M-Factor is not the same as a negative personality trait that has to change, but there is a good chance one element of her M-Factor will undergo a transformation. This is the side of your heroine that gets her into trouble, and that, nine times out of ten, will be her blind spot. By helping Josue, Dora gets a belated experience of mothering and opening up to an experience with another individual that she can't control. Dora is still Dora by the end of the story, but she's opened her eyes. I reckon she'll still be grumpy. She's not going to volunteer for a mission in a hurry. But she might think twice before not posting her clients' letters again.

Scarlett O'Hara's M-Factor: By the end of her long story, during which she is sorely tested by poverty, civil war, and her own blind spot, Scarlett does not give up her ebullient determination. She is never really going to be a truly altruistic being. But she might think twice about playing any more games with Rhett if she really wants to get him back.

EXERCISE: YOUR HEROINE'S M-FACTOR

Do the M-Factor equation in the preceding text, and see what you come up with for your heroine. Don't worry if you surprise or even shock yourself. You can always change it when further character and story development generate bigger and better insights. Once you've found your heroine's M-Factor, use it as a metaphoric touchstone. It will always bring you back to base.

Wrapping Up…

By now, you should have identified your heroine and have a good idea about her M-Factor. Now it's time to think about the role choices your heroine makes in her life.

GOING AGAINST TYPE

Chapter 3

Your heroine will have made certain choices about life when she walks onto page one of your screenplay (or not too long after, hopefully). It's up to you to decide what those choices are and how they are going to either change during her story or be cemented in her sense of identity.

The audience will make immediate assessments about your heroine based on the information you give about her. It's a human need to "place" a person as quickly as possible, so we can start to relate to them. We root out recognizable factors in characters, so we can test our worldview and our own experience against them. Even when we watch a world movie, from an entirely different culture, we look out for themes, characters, and stories that might bear out or validate our own understanding.

As with all characters, your audience will try to "place" the heroine as soon as it can. Each member of the audience will relate your heroine to their own external and internal experiences and expectations of what women are or should be like. By *external*, I mean the women they have met and related to in their own lives. By *internal* I mean the idealized image or negative projections we all carry around about women, which emerge out of our deep unconscious. The most ready-made way of helping the audience connect to the character is to use stereotypes, the most two-dimensional and clichéd form of characterization. Stereotypes and stereotypical behavior can and do have some limited uses, particularly in comedies, but as I'm sure I don't need to tell you, this is the exception rather than the rule.

In developing your heroine's character, there's a great way of making sure you avoid stereotypes and make her unique, while recognizing that a woman in the story usually triggers some pretty powerful unconscious feelings in the audience. This is done by developing and using your heroine's role choices.

> **A role choice is your heroine's conscious and unconscious relationship to cultural expectations of women's roles.**

A role choice affects your heroine's internal and external sense of identity. A good way of thinking about role choices is to relate them to stages we go through in life, when we identify with certain ways of being. It's when people say things like, "that was when I was into being a domestic goddess" or "that's the time when nothing was going to stop me," or "that's when I was trying to be a better mother than my own mom." It's the "when I was being…" bit of the statement that reflects what a role choice is and how your heroine will think about it.

As you get to know each role choice, imagine your heroine is very old, looking back over the course of her life. How would she remember these roles she took on?

ACCEPTABLE CLICHÉS AND STEREOTYPES

Thinking about your heroine's role choices will help you make a better judgment call regarding what is a recognizable and truthful aspect to her individual character and what can be a cliché. When it comes to writing women characters, we risk colluding with clichés. It can be really hard to know what is cliché and what is true to life. For screenwriters, cliché is the most dreaded form of bad writing, so why aren't we more alert to these acceptable clichés? I do it myself, so I know what I'm talking about.

The most obvious acceptable clichéd characters include good and happy mothers who never lose it with their kids, the fashionista who has to learn deeper values, the neurotic woman who has to be tamed through the love of a man, the nice girl next door, the mean girl, the career woman who learns to put others first, the supportive wife (not that wives can't be supportive but when you only see this dimension of a female character it's a cliché) and the nagging wife (vice versa), and the downtrodden victim. Do not forget all those simplistic women in adverts thinking they are worth it or who have discovered the best detergent. I often find it amusing that you can be watching great female characters on TV, like those in *The Wire*, *Weeds*, and *Damages* when the commercial break is stuffed with stereotypes.

Some acceptable clichés are even used as an argument to show how far women have come when the cliché proves the opposite! When people claim strippers and prostitutes are empowered women in control of their lives they are spouting an acceptable cliché: to justify men's sexual need for the 'oldest profession' and women's non-sexual need (usually money) to collude by selling their bodies. There simply can't be one stripper or prostitute who hasn't at some point had to face, at least to some degree, a sense of self-betrayal in doing her job. When a prostitute says she loves her job and is in control, I have one thing to say: "The lady doth protest too much, methinks." I know we've come a long way from the "tart with a heart" stereotype, and many representations of prostitutes and strippers are more dimensional, but we don't often see the prostitute's normal life or real motivations, such as low self-esteem, beyond a gratuitous or titillating outer shell.

Acceptable clichés in story action can include the heroine needing a man to sort her problem out; the ugly duckling finally realizing that she can be a beautiful woman if she makes an effort *and* loving the newfound attention; the girls' night out in which the wild spirit of women is unleashed; the wedding dress shopping session; and the woman being angry because she's been let down by her useless man — again!

There are several factors behind the enduring existence of the "acceptable cliché." First, traditional notions of what women should and shouldn't be affect all women's lives. We reject these notions, uncomfortably collude with them, or see them as normal. It can be hard to distinguish between acceptable cliché and what we really believe women can relate to. Secondly, there's the tricky business of writing a heroine and pleasing the many people you write for. Everyone in the creative process of developing a heroine is going to be concerned about her audience appeal. I'm going to talk more about this in Chapter 9, "Unsung Heroines."

Role choices are there to help you think beyond the acceptable clichés. They are drawn from roles that most cultures, including the "postfeminist" West, associate with women and that women assume. The main aim of the role choice is to help you work out how your heroine, as an individual, relates to each role choice. The more you enter your heroine's mind, the more you will understand her individual choices and actions. A role choice isn't a job or actual vocation. Your heroine's attitude to certain role choices may result in her choosing certain kinds of jobs (or being stuck with no option but to do a certain kind of job), but a role choice is much broader. It's about her whole identity and self-perception as a woman.

By using role choices creatively you can illuminate your character's individuality and the specific nature of the culture she lives within.

Beyond Archetypes

As you will soon see, using role choices to help develop character is quite different than using the Jungian archetypes. Archetypes are based on the principle that certain recognizable roles are a result of human existence and emerge out of a collective unconscious. They are seen as masks that we wear, and which are interchangeable. A role choice says, "Wait a minute, this role is culturally created!" The usual definitions of archetypes don't help you question the cultural expectations around the roles your heroine chooses. A stereotype and archetype can only go so far. A role choice asks you to define your character's choices and the reasons for them. The whole point of a role choice is to help you question the notion of "types." If someone says your heroine is a "maternal type," it could mean that you have emphasized in her character an over-identification with the nurturing role choice.

HOW TO USE ROLE CHOICES

A role choice can help you to question and explore your heroine's attitudes toward her world. In this respect, you can use a role choice to question certain expectations about women and how they play out in your story. Using role choices creatively can help you define your heroine's internal and external identity as a girl or a woman. How your heroine relates to each role choice is a way you can deepen your characterization *and* your story. They can make you question your own feelings and views about why women make certain role choices.

It is most likely that as the story develops, so will your heroine's role choices. She might strongly identify with certain role choices at the start of her story that she will gradually grow out of. She might start identifying with another. The role choice can last the whole story long or be momentary, visible in a scene or two. Your heroine can identify with any role choice at any given moment.

You might decide that certain role choices will only be evident in other female characters in order to serve as a reminder of what your heroine could be if conditions or her attitudes change or not. Seeing it in other women, for example, might make her reject that particular role choice because it's the last thing she wants to be identified with. Or another character will make a certain role choice and be a good example for the heroine.

Remember, role choices are a creative approach to support your writing choices. So treat them flexibly. There's no right or wrong.

The five groups of role choices in a heroine's story are:

- Heroine
- Nurturer
- Dependant
- Believer
- Caryatid

Each group of role choices have many varieties within each one, which you will get to know.

A Question of Age?

If it helps you, you can see the role choices as reflections of common stages of women's lives. For instance, you could see the Dependant as reflecting childhood and adolescence, the Believer as reflecting the idealism of young adults, the Nurturer as reflecting the childbearing years of women who become mothers and wives, and the Caryatid as a reflection of older women's lives when they have more freedom from family commitments. Using the role choices like this doesn't really do justice to their character-building potential. They are really based on the principle that what is a relevant choice to one woman's life isn't going to be the same for another. Age in years doesn't necessarily mean maturity of mind.

As you will find out, role choices frequently subvert our expectations, depending on the personality of the heroine making the choice. They support uniqueness and memorability. Now let's meet each one.

THE ROLE CHOICE OF HEROINE

The heroine role choice is very simple. It represents your main female character *seeking or reacting to a certain kind of life to be true to herself*. Think about it, aren't we all on a mission to make sense of our lives the best way we can? Well, your heroine is doing exactly that. In your story, you are going to narrow down a period of her life and make the "seeking" and "reacting" very specific to her and the situation she is in. To be a heroine of her own life motivates every female character in your story.

Your heroine might hate her life and want change, fall into change by accident, or want to protect the status quo. She might need to recover from pain or past trauma, so that she can move on and heal the scars. She might be frozen and spend the whole story thawing. She might want to go on an amazing quest, pursue a career, solve a riddle, or seek vengeance or justice. She might want to be extremely bad. The heroine role choice is behind all of these drives and far more. Heroine is the role choice behind every woman in the story. What kind of heroine role choices your heroine identifies with at any given moment will definitely evolve. The main different kinds of heroine are the Outsider Heroine, Incomplete Heroine, Survivor Heroine, and Questing Heroine.

Outsider Heroines

These can be misfits, rebels, lesbians, disabled women, older women, sick women, or addicted women. Their dominant drive is to *seek life on their own terms in spite of external expectations*. It's not high on these heroines' agendas to belong to society, or sometimes they have no choice in the matter if they are outcasts or just can't belong. Some Outsider Heroines have taken one look at the status quo and realized it's not for them. They don't want to belong; they are motivated to reject it, particularly if society labels them as somehow redundant or undesirable, like the three middle-aged heroines in *Heading South*, who seek sun and sex with younger men in Haiti. These women are unconventional and defiant. An Outsider Heroine is like a reverse fish-out-of-water. She jumped out of the water a long time ago and found she adapted quite well, thank you very much. It's going back in that scares her. *Cheri* shows a group of high-class Parisian prostitutes using their considerable wealth to ape the high-society lifestyle that excludes them. A heroine might hate the judgments society makes about her through no fault of her own. Sometimes, the heroine becomes an Outsider Heroine because she finally realizes she doesn't belong anymore, try as she might. She might be too old, too plain, too fat, just like the fat little sister Anais in *A Ma Soeur!*. She is never going to belong or be good enough, so why fight it?

Sometimes she might be too poor, too ethnically different as in *She, a Chinese*, a film in which the heroine struggles to belong to her own and a new culture. *Frozen River* and *Precious* both have Outsider Heroines who are also excluded by their extreme poverty and lack of opportunity. Sometimes a heroine is an Outsider for something as simple as being a "woman returner," a woman who is going back to work after years of child rearing, plagued by lack of confidence. Sometimes she's an Outsider because someone's forced her there. Kitty in *The Painted Veil* is a bourgeois and shallow woman who is dragged by her husband to a cholera-infested Chinese rural community as a punishment for infidelity. In her isolation she learns some important lessons about herself and love in the process.

Outsider Heroines don't often reintegrate into mainstream life. It can be the last thing they want anyway. But they might dip their toe into the pool of convention, just to see what they aren't missing, or so they can validate their lifestyle choices. Sometimes their outsider existence is interrupted by someone needing something from them, and they feel a moral compunction to change their ways. Dora in *Central Station* is one of these.

Every woman has something of the Outsider in her. This is the result of equality for women arriving relatively recently. Even today, many high-achieving women feel they suffer "imposter" syndrome in their jobs, even when they are successful. Even young women, who weren't born in the throes of feminism, can feel this so there must be something about being born female that still casts the outsider shadow, however faint. The woman who breastfeeds her baby in public and is asked to go to the ladies room is momentarily an Outsider Heroine. By doing the most natural thing in the world, she can fall outside expectations.

Survivor Heroines

Victims, betrayed women, entrapped women, abused women, and ex-addicted women are found in this category. Their dominant drive is to *seek life*. Sometimes life has dealt extra painful blows to a woman. She's been harshly knocked off center and needs to find her balance.

Needing to achieve closure on the past wound can be a very powerful drive in a Survivor Heroine. In *I've Loved You So Long*, Juliette needs to come to terms with her decision to end the life of her six-year-old son. Although she is also an Outsider Heroine because of her long prison incarceration, her driving need is to mourn the loss of her little boy, forgive herself, and move on. Loss and bereavement are common to Survivor Heroines, such as Holly in *P.S. I Love You*, Hannah in *The English Patient*, and Manuela in *All About My Mother* whose stories focus on their process of healing the deepest pain.

The scars of romantic love are very common in Survivor Heroines. Infidelity, cruel rejection, being forced to give up one's true love, and the opposite, the arranged marriage, are all frequent motivations for the heroine to recover from the past and seek a new life.

Survivor Heroines' stories tend to have powerful arcs in which a heroine starts in one state and ends the narrative in a much better place, at least mentally. Sometimes there is no way of surviving a brutal regime that is designed to crush its heroines. *The Circle* and the *Curse of the Golden Flower*, both Fighting Femininity films, have heroines who end up mentally or physically annihilated. Sometimes a heroine seeks life in the face of death. *My Life Without Me*, *Frida*, and *Sylvia* all follow heroines with a tenuous grip on life. Survival for these heroines means keeping it together in spite of the threat of death.

None of us go through life protected from loss, pain, or injury. The process of recovery from loss includes denial, despair, numbness, guilt, and anger. Surviving Heroines experience all these emotions and more. With these heroines you can fray your audience's nerves and redden their eyes. *Precious* takes us on a rollercoaster ride in which her path to autonomy from a position of complete victimization is harrowing yet ultimately transcendental.

Incomplete Heroines

Rejected women, women yearning for love, women who do not feel emotionally whole, women with mental health problems, and women who love too much are all Incomplete Heroines. The dominant drive of this role choice is *to seek emotional fulfilment*.

Most romantic heroines fall into this category. These are women who seek balance in their relationships and need to work on their issues to heal their relationship problems. Historical heroines such as Scarlett O'Hara in *Gone with the Wind* and Ida in *Cold Mountain*, to very contemporary heroines like Carrie Bradshaw in *Sex in the City* and Amanda and Iris in *The Holiday* embark on very emotional and internal journeys to make sense of their relationships. They need to heal internal wounds that are getting in the way of either their own personal autonomy or their ability to find love.

The love interest of an Incomplete Heroine is usually her best healer and teacher, but sometimes they can represent her deepest pain. I explain the reciprocal nature of love relationships in Chapter 7, "Making Love and Feeling Good," but it's important to emphasize the role of The Other person in an Incomplete Heroine's life. If there are problems in her relationships, it's usually down to an unresolved problem or an internal wound that is crying out to be healed. The relationship either needs to end or grow. The Incomplete Heroine has to face up to the fact that although life may have dealt her some blows, until she takes responsibility for her pain, she will not recover. Kym in *Rachel Getting Married* leaves rehab pretending that she's dealt with her drug addiction. It emerges that not only is she lying about her progress to everyone, but also she's lying to herself. Her deepest pain is the fact that her drug taking led to her little brother's death when he was in her care. Completeness can only be gained for Kym by going back into rehab and truly facing herself and owning her responsibility.

A Survivor Heroine, who has endured unbearable loss, sometimes identifies with the Incomplete Heroine when she has achieved closure but is left feeling empty inside. It's like the desolation after the storm. Now the actual trauma has taken place, the rebuilding needs to begin.

Of all the different ways a character can identify with a role choice, probably the Incomplete Heroine is the most frequent. We all have inadequacies, insecurities, losses, hang-ups, and unfulfilled needs. From "shopaholicism" to sex addiction, we can compensate for inner emptiness in many ways. An Incomplete Heroine's problems tend to dominate her story. Her inner need is her true goal.

Questing Heroines

Leaders, saints, seekers of justice, police investigators and lawyers, warriors, vengeance seekers, and murderers are the most obvious types of questing heroines. Quests can be creative, physical, occupational, spiritual, and medical, anything where a tangible result can be achieved by effort and tenacity. The drive of these heroines is to *seek a result* in the outside world. They have clear external goals that drive their story. These heroines dominate the genres in which high stakes are everything. If the heroine doesn't solve the problem, there will be more deaths, wars, corruption, and bad guys having their way. Sometimes the quests are relatively small in scope but not significance. In *Julie and Julia*, both Julie and Julia are heroines who are feeling incomplete and unfulfilled. Julia Child is an embassy official's wife with too much time on her hands in Paris, and Julie has a harrowing day job and a big sense of failure in comparison to her high-achieving girlfriends. Julia goes on a quest to learn cooking, leading her to fulfil her ambition of having her French cookery book published. Julie goes on a quest to write a blog, using Julia Child's entire recipe collection over a year.

Often Questing Heroines are queens who seek to retain power against insurmountable odds. Elizabeth I in *Elizabeth* and Victoria in *The Young Victoria* embark on quests to prove themselves as worthy monarchs. The loss of anything resembling a normal woman's life may lead them to feeling incomplete, but the quest is a dominant drive in them.

As they develop leadership skills during the quest, we watch them grow into legendary women.

TV is full of Questing Heroines in any crime-related genre, for example, *CSI: Crime Scene Investigation*, *Medium*, *Damages*, and *Weeds*. Even the *Desperate Housewives* have a mission to find out the truth about their friend's death in season 1. There's always a huge amount of learning on the job, and many of them begin as Outsider Heroines or Incomplete Heroines before they find their quest.

The morality of the Questing Heroine can often be a big question. Do her means justify her ends? Does she compromise or sacrifice her true nature in order to obtain her desired result? Then there is the common inner female conflict of being too many things to too many people. Can she meet the domestic and relationship needs of loved ones as well as the external task? Maria in *Maria Full of Grace* rejects the universal demands on her as sister, daughter, provider, and employee in order to try and meet her own needs. Conventional notions of heroism can be upheld by the Questing Heroine, more so than any other heroine role choice, where "saving the self" can often come before saving others. But even for the highest-minded heroines, there's usually a sting in the tail of heroism. Take Erin in *Erin Brockovich*. If she saves a community, she will fail her family. Which does she sacrifice?

Your heroine will relate to the Questing Heroine when she gives herself a mission. How she goes about achieving it will depend on her needs and sense of identity.

Tip for Writing the Heroine Role Choice

Think about how your heroine might start out as one kind of heroine, and as she resolves issues, she evolves into another kind of heroine. Remember *Precious*? She starts out as a Survivor and Outsider, but ends up as a Questing Heroine, determined to get her children and bring them up on her terms. Rose in *Titanic* starts out as a Questing Heroine on the boat, goes back in time to being an Incomplete Heroine needing love, and ends up a Survivor as the boat sinks. Back to the present again, Rose's quest to feel reunited with Jack is fulfilled.

The Heroine Role Choice in Close-Up

La Vie en Rose

Edith is in a small French town's square with her father, who is performing contortionist tricks to get enough money for food and shelter that night. Edith is a Survivor and Outsider Heroine, whose very life has been threatened by deprivation ever since birth. The townspeople are laughing at her father, much to Edith's humiliation, and his act is not attracting many tips. When someone asks her father if his little girl performs, Edith squirms with fear about exposure. Sensing a chance to make more money, Edith's father urgently orders her to do something fast, before the crowd disperses. In a fit of panic, Edith sings *La Marsellaise*, with a beautiful and clear voice. Soon the crowd is mesmerized and deeply impressed. As the townspeople dig deep in their pockets for Edith, the little girl is flooded with her first-ever feeling of pride and achievement. Edith has found her talent, one that will make her Edith Piaf. Later, as a drug-addicted adult and an Incomplete Heroine, she will always rely on her talent to help her feel whole.

THE ROLE CHOICE OF NURTURER

Women "mother." It's what we are all trained to do from day one. And "mothering" — loving, feeding, cleaning, tending, caring, and being totally alert and immediately responsive to the needs of others — is the essential job description for the role choice of Nurturer. Out of all the role choices, it has the most powerful influence over women's lives. The role choice of Nurturer is when your heroine puts another character or other characters' needs first, often at the expense of her own. As women are conditioned by culture to do this without blinking, this role choice is central to most heroines' sense of identity. But this doesn't mean your heroine is necessarily any good at it, or even enjoys it! How to look after her own needs can be a woman's biggest dilemma.

The Nurturer includes mothers, childcare workers, caretakers, nurses, or anyone whose role, vocation, or motivation is to tend to the emotional and physical needs of others. A heroine chooses the role choice of Nurturing for a variety of reasons, such as the need to build a family, have a certain job, or simply be the one that everyone turns to for emotional support and care taking. Nurturing can be pleasurable, satisfying, or the complete opposite for your heroine. She might buck against the expectation to look after others and be completely hopeless, or she might take it in her stride and accept it as one of her normal roles in life. The two main different kinds of Nurturer are Mother and Sorority.

Mother

The universal expectation for women to mother is exactly why heroines who are mothers very often lead stories that focus on being a mother. Her parenting is central to the story and her characterization. The heroine who happens to be a mother but has a story that has nothing to do with her being a parent is a rare creature. In the op-posite direction, a childless female character over forty years old who doesn't have any issues about not having children is equally absent on our screens. In the vast majority of stories, a heroine/mother's whole identity is bound up with her mothering. Whether you think that women are the natural caretakers, or if you believe the expectations of women to do the lion's share of the hands-on parenting are simply a division of gender roles, your attitude as writer is going to filter down into your characterization. So it's good to be aware of some the issues. The role choice of Mother will mean very different things to a character that is young and immature with no interest in nurturing her baby like Sherry in *SherryBaby* to an infertile woman in her forties like Julia Child in *Julie and Julia*.

Loving It

There's always the overwhelming feeling of love when a heroine and her partner are ready to have a child and create a family. One of my favorite movie moments is the Mr. Napkin Head scene in *The Holiday,* in which Amanda discovers that the man she is deeply attracted to is a widower with two young daughters. As they all drink cocoa and joke around at the table, the subtext is all about Amanda's emotional ability to let these two little girls into her life by becoming their stepmom. If you believe in the primitive maternal instinct or not, the intense joy of being a parent is undeniable. It is the hardest job, but it is also the most rewarding. Most women and men do their best for their children, even when their best falls short. The adaptation to the role choice of Mother is long and all-consuming; the call to love and protect her children will change your heroine's identity and life forever more.

A Difficult Job

To cope with mothering well, a woman needs emotional and practical support, and someone looking out for her needs. But how often does this happen, in reality? In stories, hardly ever! A woman's capacity to be a good mother is either idolized (*Changeling*) or demonized (every film with a bad mother, of which there are many). Every human being needs a nurturer, and those who mother others need it most. In our society, who cares for the caretaker? How do mothers — or men who mother — get their needs met? Stories are coming round to acknowledge the real challenges of motherhood. In *Monsters Ball*, Letitia takes her misery out on her son. In *Mamma Mia!* Donna is burnt out by years of single motherhood and "nurturing" her hotel and her daughter, but she has no one to look after her needs. *Something's Gotta Give* explores the dilemma of the older heroine who is a mother. She is fancied by a younger man while she is forming an unconscious attraction to a man her own age who has been dating her daughter!

Mothering, unsupported and isolated, is bad for a woman's mental health. We were supposed to raise children in communities, not lonely domestic units. It's a known fact that in nations where women can earn money, live autonomously, and have control over their fertility, the birth rate drops. Women's needs in coping with motherhood can be played down on screen, so watch out for romanticizing or gorgonizing your heroine/mother by making her responsible for all her children's hang-ups.

If you're writing a heroine/mother, think outside the box of received wisdom to make her memorable or real. In *The Edge of Love*, about Dylan Thomas' two great loves, the tiny children of the two heroines are in practically every scene. The film is surprisingly truthful about the drudgery and exhaustion of having a child on your hip all day, and the support that women have to give each other. On the upside, *Weeds* has a great deal of fun with the challenges of a multitasking widowed single mom of two sons, while she runs a marijuana drug-dealing business.

Maternal Guilt

You might want to explore this aspect of your heroine's identity as a mother because every mother feels it! The pressure to mother well is huge and often unrealistic. Women can feel there's something wrong with them if they aren't very good at it. Most mothers have bad days, resent their children, and take stress out in fits of maternal meltdown. Nobody wants to lose it but almost everybody does. It's a logical response to a situation in which you have to take care of everyone else first. This is a major issue for most women, as *The Rebound* shows, when a single mom realizes her young son walks in on her having sex with a man he doesn't know. *Divine Secrets of the Ya-Ya Sisterhood* show a mother burdened with maternal guilt for years because she was an alcoholic and abusive to her children. *The Duchess* shows a mother unable to leave her children to be with her supportive lover despite her horrible life with her cold husband.

Biology of Mothering

Child birth is hardly ever written in an empowering way, a way in which a woman takes control of her own processes. Lots of women squat, kneel, go deeply inward, talk to the baby, and do stretching exercises with partners helping them, but these images are more likely to be seen on a documentary about indigenous women than your local multiplex on a Saturday night. Birthing in the West has been overmedicalized so a heroine lying back and screaming with a medical gown has become the acceptable cliché. Birth is sometimes shot from the women's point of view, but more often it is not. For something really extreme (and funny) check out the birth scenes in *TranSylvania* in which three filthy gypsies brandish a dirty knife between the legs of the terrified heroine.

Infertility is a deeply felt wound in women and men. In a world that glorifies motherhood through a bombardment of media images, it is hard for the infertile woman not to be reminded daily about her plight or to consider herself a failure or, worse, an outsider. A fertility-challenged character is Julia Child's in *Julie and Julia*. Her passion for cooking could be a compensatory need to nurture, but Nora Ephron's characterization does not stigmatize Julia's infertility.

Stepmoms

They have a really raw deal in stories. As the number of step-moms probably increases every day, it's time for some new visions. For a start, many birth mothers do have "issues" with the fact that the father of their children has moved on. This can lead to women sabotaging — consciously or unconsciously — their children's relationship with a stepmom, as in *Stepmom*. Some birth mothers justify this by believing they are simply protecting their children from something that might threaten their stability, but sometimes it can be about loss of power and a need to get back at the ex. The worse-case scenario is when a father is alienated from his children because of the mother's propaganda. The evil stepmother of fairytales could just be the unfair recipient of negative projections for centuries. Where are the men while the battle rages? Often they are somewhere in the middle, trying to keep both sides happy.

This is not to say that some stepmoms can be highly inadequate, jealous, and insecure. They might exclude the children from the new life and make them feel like second-class citizens. It might suit a stepmom very well that her man's baggage from the past is out of sight. If the children are lucky, they will have a mature mother and stepmother who understand relationships are a two-way process.

Rejecting It

Whatever your views on abortion, it's still a story taboo. Isn't there some irony about the silence and fear around the issue when so many masculine stories condone the taking of life, such as torture, murder, and death? But many women have abortions, and probably every woman in the West knows someone close who's had one. Like all taboos, the lid blows off at some point, due to the rising pressure of being ignored. In recent years abortion has been explored in *Vera Drake*, *4 Months, 3 Weeks and 2 Days*, and now *The Edge of Love*. Out of the three, *The Edge of Love* is the most down to Earth. One woman lends another money for the operation, and then comes round after to support her. It's all set in 1940s Wales, and the whole thing is illegal, but it is done without any stigmatization.

If you are writing about an abortion decision faced by your heroine, and she goes through with it, you will have to confront all your paranoia about her likability and the unlikely odds of it ever making it to the screen. Even if abortion only features in your heroine's backstory, it's useful to know how your heroine would handle an unwanted pregnancy and who would support her.

Abandoners

If your heroine has for whatever reason decided to abandon her children, you risk working in cliché-infested waters or being something of a pioneer if you just keep it in her backstory. Women, for a whole variety of personal reasons, flee the family nest. Some never come back. It's generally okay to have a male hero who has some kids in the background. His lack of involvement may not be a major issue for him. It's not the same for heroine/mothers. But there are many women who don't feel able to raise their children. Sometimes issues from childhood are reawakened when a mother has children, and these seriously undermine her capacity to care. Some women have full-scale psychotic breakdowns after birth and never develop a deep bond with their child. The mother who left and it's no big heartache or not central to her story is an exceptionally rare breed. She doesn't have to be unlikeable, maybe things just didn't work out. Maybe her ex was the better nurturer. It is still a huge deal for women to leave their children, so central to a woman's identity is the role of Nurturer.

Sorority

The Sorority is shorthand for the huge variety of female collectives and your heroine's need (or not) to be part of a group of females. The role choice of Sorority is a regular feature in heroines' stories because it represents women's need to share, empathize, connect, and feel understood. Women can have strong needs to communicate and affiliate, more than men. Women can have an intuitive empathy with each other, even if they don't like to admit it.

Your task with the Sorority role choice is to work out if your heroine feels a need to sometimes be with other women to give and get emotional support. Does she have a sorority in her life and how does she relate to it? You can see the role choice of Sorority in all genres from comedies to thrillers.

Supportive Sorority

This is the bunch of friends who pat your heroine on the back, listen to her woes, lick her wounds, and put her back on her feet. They are the friends to whom your heroine can bare her soul and not feel judged. They probably know her better than she knows herself. They know all your heroine's past boyfriends and will patiently listen to all her relationship trials and tribulations. They are there for your heroine, whatever time of the day or night. The Sorority role choice is often found in comedies, romantic comedies, dramantic comedies, and dramedies. Obviously *Sex and the City* is based on this role choice as the four friends need each other as much as their relationships with men. But the Supportive Sorority isn't all a bed of roses. Because they know your heroine so well, they can also give her a hard time. Or, love of a man can come between members, and suddenly they become rivals. Female friendships can get incredibly intense because of this ability to share and open up but can turn nasty quite quickly.

Campaigning and Protective Sororities

If you believe that women don't have equal status in society, then you might want to show your heroine making the Sorority role choice in order to empower herself, particularly when she's been treated badly by men. She might seek out a protective Sorority to help her. Then there are all the women-led organizations to support women such as incest, rape, and domestic violence survivor groups. Your heroine may need one of these or may have experienced the support of one of these in her backstory. Women's political groups abound. The women of most countries wouldn't have the right to vote without the struggles and sacrifices of organized groups of women. If you're a female writer, you might well be a member of *Women in Film and TV,* which aims to break down the glass ceiling in our industry.

Educational Sororities

Your heroine might go to a girls' school. The single-sexed education system is a frequent subject of heroine's stories in the U.K., where I'm from. Stories include *The Prime of Miss Jean Brodie, St. Trinian's, An Education,* and *Cracks* to name just a few. Why? Because girls' schools are part of our cultural heritage. Educational Sororities expose the intensity of female relationships, and their more unpleasant side, like passive-aggressive behavior, bitchiness, and cliques. They are fascinating no-man's worlds that have a powerful influence on young women's developing minds.

Enforced Sororities

Your heroine might find herself stuck with a sorority and no way out. Just like the child widow in *Water*, she's condemned to an isolated life with other Indian widows. The harem and entrapping brothel is another version of this, as in *Memoirs of a Geisha*. Women are bonded by sexual slavery, which can produce empathy as well as rivalry.

Institutional Sororities

Along with girls' schools, convents are the most obvious form of organized sororities. The difference is that nuns have elected to be there for life. The nuns in *Sister Act* have to adapt to an outside element coming in, in the form of a wild, sexual, and liberated woman who shows them a new and progressive way of performing.

Historical Sororities

These reflect historical periods when women's lack of power in the outside world meant that they had to spend most of their time with other women. From ladies-in-waiting to below-stairs servant girls, women have lived among each other for most of their lives.

Real Sororities

There are far more movies about adult sisters who live together rather than adult brothers, or adult sisters and brothers (the French film *Female Agents* proved a good exception to this, and is definitely worth seeing as it also shows an enforced sorority). *In Her Shoes, Hilary and Jackie, Ladies in Lavender*, and *The Other Boleyn Girl* all explore the conflicts and primary bond between blood sisters. The rivalry, intense envy, and overt or covert hostility between these sisters are contradicted by a sense of unconditional connection without boundaries. In *Hilary and Jackie*, Hilary du Pre lets her sister Jacqueline sleep with her own husband because she cannot say no to her and somehow feels responsible for her. Your heroine can't choose a blood bond, but she can choose how she relates to her sister. In *The Secret Life of Bees*, the Boatwright sisters choose to be together for love, protection, and unity in a racist world.

Tips for Writing the Nurturer Role Choice

Male Nurturers

You are doing your bit for the human race when you create male nurturing characters who are the true caretakers of others. Some men are just better nurturers than women, and you don't have to make a big deal out of it in your story. As more men take on the caregiving role it will be less of an issue when a male character is the stay-at-home dad. In many close relationships, both partners share the nurturing role at different times. This kind of parental teamwork is evident in the TV show *Medium* and, more famously, between Miranda and Steve in *Sex and the City*.

Female Bonding

Remember women can sometimes be too nice to each other. It can be difficult to hurt your best friend. A group of women friends is nurturing because everybody's so empathetic. Subtext in female bonding scenes can work really well to show the real dynamics between women, which they are often too afraid of communicating.

Characterizing the Sorority

How you characterize the sorority will help you avoid acceptable clichés. Create quirky and different characters in the group who stand out with a meaningful function to the story.

The Nurturer Role Choice in Close-Up

Paris je t'aime

Ana is an illegal immigrant nanny for a rich Parisian woman. Ana has to put her baby into terrible day care for long hours to care for the other woman's child. She then has to travel by a congested train through the suburbs of Paris to get to an upscale sixteenth arrondissement where she works. Her rich employee has absolutely no interest in finding out whether Ana has her own childcare responsibilities and tells her she's going to be late that night. Ana thinks she has no right to ask to leave on time. When the baby she looks after starts to cry, Ana sings a song and comforts it, all the time imagining her own. As night falls, she has no way of knowing what is happening to her own child now that the nursery has closed.

This scene shows that the way women nurture is not always a matter of choice. A poor woman might be the better mother, but she can't bring her own child up. Wealth might mean material comfort, but it may also mean emotional deprivation. *The Nanny Diaries* is a comedy that explores extreme competitiveness between rich Manhattan mothers, which is even more important to them than their children's emotional well-being.

THE ROLE CHOICE OF DEPENDANT

Some heroines are dependent on others, or they choose this way of being. Others are literally at the mercy of others and have no other choice. Then there are those who convince themselves that they are helpless in order to fulfill a deep psychological need to be looked after by others. "Kept woman" is still a more common platitude than "kept man," but times are changing.

The Dependant role choice comes from centuries of women having very little economic or political power. Up until relatively recently in the history of the world, women and children were part of a man's property. Even the categories of Mrs., Miss, and Ms. are a hangover from times in which marital status defined a woman's identity. The role choices of Dependant are Child, Victim, and Supportee.

Child

Some heroines are children, and by their very status are dependent on the care of others. Children have no power in our culture and therefore little responsibility. Maturity is all about becoming responsible for yourself and others who depend on you. Some adult heroines, however, reflect the role choice of Child because they don't want to grow up. They might be happy with having the power, but they certainly don't want responsibility. Scarlett O'Hara is infuriating because she will not grow up. During her story she has to face some situations in which she has to put others first, but she does it out of grim necessity, not because of any real desire or mending of her ways. Other heroine/children have too much responsibility for their young age and have their childhoods stolen from them. Although they can be old for their years, when they are adults they may have arrested development as they permanently try to recapture a lost youth. When these children become adults (or even earlier) and discover drugs, the "hit" can allow the mind a surge of release that feels too good to lose. They literally get their lost childhoods back in one hit. You can see this kind of arrested development in Edith Piaf in *La Vie en Rose*. Edith's childhood was deprived on every level, with a drunken mother and a cold father. The childlike part of Edith makes her impulsive, demanding, and addicted to heroin. If she nurtures anything it is her talent, but even that she abuses.

In *SherryBaby*, Sherry wants to regain custody of her daughter after leaving prison, but she's still a child herself and an addict. It's very common for the childlike heroine to have issues with parenting. How can she be a good enough parent, when she's still a child herself? Sherry and Edith both can't handle the Mother role choice, and both feel guilty but find it virtually impossible to change.

The heroine who is a child at heart does at least show the ability to receive from others. This is actually her strength — to a point. The problem arises for this kind of heroine because she likes to receive in a relationship but not do too much of the giving. If for any reason her codependent "providing" partner can't fulfill his role, and needs her to look after him, the relationship can suddenly be at risk.

Ms. Bright Side

Free-spirited heroines who are always chasing rainbows can be highly charismatic, with oodles of M-Factor. Retaining a childlike ability to explore, this kind of heroine recognizes no limits and has an endless sense of wonder. If your heroine has these gifts, her freedom can be exhilarating not only for her but also for the audience. Take Amelia Earhart in *Amelia*, Sugar in *Some Like It Hot*, and Samantha in *Sex and the City* for example, we want to have fun with these heroines and see the world through their eyes. They are often optimists, thrill seekers, and risk takers. We want them to live their dreams, not be crushed by the system.

Victim

If your heroine identifies with the role choice of Victim it will be because she is at the mercy of another person's power or a social system has power over her. Alternatively, she will be identifying as a Victim to be able to manipulate another person into looking after her by "playing the victim." Quite a range, isn't it?

Vulnerable Victims

Being a vulnerable kind of Victim is not something any heroine is likely to choose for herself, but it is a kind of role choice. Why? Because nine times out of ten, the only person who can help the heroine out of this situation is herself. I'm not talking about how the countless masculine-oriented films wind up in the third act with the male hero saving a helpless and endangered woman (who is often very beautiful). These female characters only end up dependent on their saviors! The reality is that women, just like men, need to empower themselves in order to feel that they are really mistresses of their own lives, it's that simple. In addition, not all men want the burden of responsibility. This aspect of masculinity, the expectation to be the provider, protector, and savior, feels as much as a trap to them as being protected feels for some women. It's better to see the need to be vulnerable as a human need. We all need to feel cared for and looked after, but sometimes we convince ourselves we can't help ourselves depending on our frame of mind or other psychological factors.

Sexual Victims

Precious in *Precious* is a Victim on almost every level of her life. She is abused by both parents, emotionally, physically, and sexually. She is African American, so she belongs to a minority group, and is female. She is obese to the point of being seriously unhealthy and is bullied in the outside world. She is barely articulate. To cap it all, she finds out she is HIV positive, thanks to repeatedly being raped by her father. In short, she is bottom of the heap and faces almost insurmountable obstacles.

Playing the Victim

This is a psychologically complicated role choice. In a culture that gives mixed messages about women's power, it's not surprising that some women use helplessness and dependency to get other people to do what they want. It's a culture-given cop-out that is complicated by the fact that men are physically stronger than women. Part of a man's moral development is learning responsibility for this power. Women have to come to terms with the fact that they are weaker. Other women genuinely feel they are helpless. A deep fear of failure or lack of confidence can prevent some women from actualizing their dreams. By convincing themselves that life is against them, they can avoid taking responsibility.

Other victims habitually live in the blaming mode. If they make everybody else responsible for their terrible lives, then they don't have to look within. This dynamic is pathological in some heroines who blame their husbands for everything wrong in their lives. An interesting example of a bitter "victim" is Terry Ann, the mother in *The Upside of Anger* who believes her husband has left her. Later Terry discovers her abandoning husband in fact died alone, accidentally. Terry's quickness to judge, blame, and resent is her striking M–Factor that drives the film.

Many heroines' stories show a transformation in the main character, emerging from a victim-like status to taking responsibility for her own life, such as Jenna in *Waitress*. Although her elderly male friend in the restaurant leaves Jenna a huge amount of money, you don't think Jenna is being saved by him. She's earned it because she has empowered herself, with the help of her female friends, to free herself from a life and an attitude that keeps her down. If your heroine is on this path, try to work out to what extent she might collude with being a victim and the reasons in the backstory that may have created her as a victim in the first place.

Supportee

Being a Supportee doesn't necessarily mean your heroine is a victim. It means she might have a genuine need for support from others, or she's chosen circumstances so that others look after her. As independent as a heroine is, there are times she will need emotional, physical, and financial support. One obvious example is after childbirth when women need care and attention. Your heroine might be bad at accepting support because she's fiercely independent, or she laps it up. She may have been brought up with the expectation that women are looked after by men. Why do some heroines want to be "kept" while others wouldn't be seen dead doing the washing and cooking? Possibly your dependant heroine has a deep-seated fear of her own strength or has lost confidence in her own abilities. She may be genuinely helpless if she was brought up to be looked after one day. It's an acceptable cliché in stories to see the aristocratic rich woman humbled by having to live like everyone else. Alternatively, some women dream of being a Supportee because there is too much domestic drudgery in their lives.

Economic dependency can be a real option for your heroine, psychologically and materially, if her husband's rich enough. Alternatively, she might come from a culture in which it's customary for the woman not to work as it's a sign of weakness of the man. There can be dogma about women and work in countries where it is assumed that mothers should raise children full-time. This doesn't mean it is normal or natural, or even good for women and children. It can simply be a cultural expectation in a particular culture. Sometimes when circumstances mean that a female Supportee has to take over the provider role, it can bring shame on the family.

Some heroines remain deskilled, undereducated, and dependent for life on their husband or children. *Brick Lane* showed a benign dictatorship of a Bangladeshi marriage, with heroine Nazreen having to deal with her unemployed husband's ego as she slowly starts to work. Going to work and earning an income coincides with the gradual breakdown of her marriage, but who can watch *Brick Lane* and say it is a bad thing? We are willing Nazreen to have some power over her own life.

The most glamorous bunch of Supportees in recent times are the ladies of Wisteria Lane, the *Desperate Housewives*. Okay, some of them do work. But the show takes a satirical peek at a sorority that is predominantly Supportees.

Tips for Writing the Dependant Role Choice

Irritation with Your Passive Heroine

It can be annoying to write your heroine being completely out of touch with herself, for instance, if she's self-pitying or passive through too much abuse. You can be screaming inside "for Christ sakes, just walk out!" This is good stuff on the whole, because it will ultimately reveal the extent of her arc. So let her drive you nuts!

Reducing Predictability

When you watch a film with a heroine who starts off in a very bad place, it's easy to predict that she's going to resolve, if not all, most of her problems. It's like a lonely heroine needing love. We often want happy endings of survival, triumph, and empowerment, but sometimes if you don't tick all the boxes of resolution it can give your audience a deeper experience and a more memorable story. Your task is to make everything that happens from beginning to end as unpredictable and memorable as possible.

Man as Savior

Remember, your heroine will always be more memorable if she plays a big part in saving herself. A loving man or friend will help her do that. He won't do it for her. Elizabeth in *Pride and Prejudice* is "saved" by Darcy on numerous levels. But she can only reap the reward of true love with her soul mate if she develops humility and an ability to see that she was wrong. Ask yourself if you truly believe women need and want to be saved or looked after by men or is this a legacy of thousands of years of having little or no economic power and being the main carer of children? How are your beliefs unconsciously influencing the outcomes for your female and male characters?

The Dependant Role Choice in Close-Up

Precious

Precious is raped by her father, while her mother watches, not preventing him or protecting her daughter. Where does she go in her mind when she's being violated? A fantasy world, where fairy god-mothers reign supreme and where Precious is adored by a gorgeous hunk who will do anything for her. For Victim Precious, the hunk is her knight in shining armor who adores her. Precious' fantasy is a coping mechanism that might temporarily alleviate pain and humiliation but does nothing to really help her get out of her harrowing situation. Only by saving herself will she be able to protect herself and her children from the clutches of her dysfunctional family.

THE ROLE CHOICE OF BELIEVER

Whether they are driven by love, ideology, revolution, or religion, heroines who reflect the role choice of Believer have a cause. Some-times their convictions serve selfish reasons, but more often than not these are altruistic individuals who want to better the cause of man- and womankind. These are women who have made this role choice because they are ideological beings at heart. They want to improve the world and make it a better place. They can handle necessary sacrifices for their cause, and they aren't scared of conflict, obstacles, or difficulty. They can be driven and workaholic, whether they go about life quietly or with a bang. The role choices of Believer are Healer, Amazon, Lover, and Rival.

Healer

Your heroine might fulfill the role choice of Believer through her healing capacities, where she tends to the physical and mental ills of another character in order to bring about change and new life. It can be a job she has in the story (doctor, nurse, midwife, drug dealer) or simply a way of being that brings about a positive change in others during the course of the story. Healers tend to be people with a strong conviction to bring about change for the good in others. It is this commitment to change that puts them in this group rather than the Nurturing group, who are more about emotional and physical *giving* of themselves. Healers understand they have a role, a duty, and they tend to make sacrifices so they can fulfill these roles and duties effectively. They basically believe they can do good and bring about change in a sick person or system.

Heroine healers come from a noble lineage of persecuted women. For several hundred years witches were burnt at the stake for offering alternative remedies that the establishment saw as subversive. The natural healthcare that is big business today ironically has its roots in intolerance and fear.

Your heroine can't heal half-heartedly. It's a job that requires total dedication or her patient will suffer. Sometimes healers ease the transition to death. Hannah in *The English Patient* nurses her badly burned patient in a bombed Italian ruin so that he won't suffer the pain of the army trucks bouncing along the mine-infested Italian roads. Juliette, the grieving mother, in *I've Loved You So Long* is a Nurturer and a Believer when she takes her sick son's life. She then needs the healing love of her devoted sister Lea to help her out of her numb depression.

Very often Believers' actions are a consequence of their own wounds. Your heroine's loss of everything meaningful to her can either result in disillusion or believing. If she believes, it's because she wants to spare others the misery or pain she has endured. She might throw herself into healing as a way of binding her own wounds. Lily in *The Secret Life of Bees* is a Dependant — a Child and a Victim — who feels acute pain for killing her mother by accident. She is healed by the sorority of the Boatwright sisters, where August Boatwright becomes a mother figure to her. Even honey is symbolic in the film as a form of herbal medicine.

Food, although an obvious form of nurture, has a strong healing capacity for some Believer Heroines. Babette in *Babette's Feast* heals a barren and cold community using her sumptuous dishes. In *The Holiday*, Iris puts all her energy into improving an old man's life. Seeing his lonely half-finished meal on a tray in his sitting room, Iris invites Arthur to a restaurant. Before you know it, she's healing his loneliness and frailty by throwing dinner parties, organizing exercise regimes, and offering friendship. In return Arthur is healing Iris's low self-esteem. Healing can often be a reciprocal process.

Your heroine might briefly stop to heal another during the course of her story. It could be a symbolic gesture of help to another that represents a change in your heroine or foreshadows a greater turning point to come.

Amazon

Believer Heroines who fight for the causes of equality and liberty as heroines are Amazons. These women are all about taking a stand for their cause, even if the cause is to live life as women on their own terms. Making this type of Believer role choice usually indicates your heroine is angry about some kind of injustice or oppression. She could take a stand for herself or on behalf of others, such as her family, other women, or another vulnerable group. Amazons tend to be galvanizers who want social change and are prepared to fight for it. Usually family commitments are second to her priority of protesting. Women wouldn't have the vote if some women hadn't abandoned their family lives to fight for suffrage. If there's one adjective to describe an Amazonian Heroine it is "empowered."

Outsider Amazons

Sometimes Amazons have to be Outsider Heroines as well because the world isn't willing to accept their vision. They can be artists, writers, teachers, or creatives of all kinds. Dian Fossey stood up for gorillas' rights and ended up being killed in *Gorillas in the Mist*. Many Amazons are acutely aware of injustice against women, such as Virginia

Woolf in *The Hours*, another Amazon for whom it all became too much. Erin in *Freedom Writers* empowers at-risk high school kids to raise their expectations beyond a life of gang culture by writing their own stories. Katherine Ann tries to motivate her female students to be far more than 1950s housewives in *Mona Lisa Smile*.

Driven Amazons

Sometimes contemporary Amazons are compensating for an inadequacy they perceived in their family. This might motivate them to become almost invincible, as they go from success to success in the outside world. This can lead them to being unable to express vulnerability or become overstressed as they have too many balls in the air. But remember the high-achieving man who is driven tends not to be judged on his inability to be vulnerable. He is generally admired and his endeavors in the world praised, despite the toll. "They have taken too much on" tends to be used about women more than men. Watch out your film doesn't collude with these unconscious and sexist expectations of women to fall apart if they are too driven in the work place. Let them succeed and do what they have to do.

Your heroine with Amazonian tendencies might also be under pressure from her family to do and give less to others. A true Amazon will bring into her relationship all her values and will be alert to her own collusion with double standards. Carrie Bradshaw has a dash of the Amazon by writing her column and exposing the sexual hypocrisy in Manhattan.

Unwitting Amazons

A heroine can become an Amazon by chance. Her eyes can slowly be opened to injustice by being plunged into an oppressive situation. In *4 Months, 3 Weeks and 2 Days*, Otilia has no choice but to help her Dependant friend Gabi through an illegal abortion during a long, harrowing night in which she becomes a lone Amazon as she faces up to a dangerous side of being a woman. In *Volver*, heroine Raimunda's quest is similar, as she has to hide the body of her abusive husband. Her daughter sees new sides to her mother as a fearless and determined protector. In *Monster*, Aileen is a tragically misguided Amazon as she pathologically murders men for their sexual transgressions. Every woman has something of the Amazon in her, whether she knows it or not. Give your heroine her Amazonian gifts with pride!

Gorgons

A stereotypical opposite of the Amazon is the Gorgon. She's a parody of the strong woman and is characterized as nagging wives, brutal schoolmistresses like Miss Trunchball in *Matilda*, and psychopaths like Annie Wilkes in *Misery*. These women are loners and they get a perverse pleasure out of making their victims suffer.

Lover

If your heroine is devoted to her love, it makes her a very special kind of Believer. Love will motivate her to make sacrifices, withstand long absences, or even permanently give up her family. Love is a healer, catalyst, and revolution all in one. It can burn and soothe. It will permanently change your heroine's life, even if it has to end. If a heroine loves, it tends to be the engine driving her entire story.

Tragic Lovers

Love for your heroine is tragic when it is doomed, destructive, or dark. If doomed, you might be interested in the obstacles that threaten and ultimately destroy love. These can be external, the stuff of eternal classics like *Brief Encounter*, *The English Patient*, and *Cold Mountain*. Alternatively, it can be the internal and self-destructive sides of a heroine that jeopardize her chance of love. She might be too needy, jealous, insecure, or too controlling, manipulative, and dangerous. No woman really wants to hear "Frankly, my dear, I don't give a damn," but often a heroine's difficult behavior can often incur such lack of sentiment. In *Mrs. Parker and the Vicious Circle*, Dorothy Parker's inner demons externally manifest as clinginess, dependency, and self-pity, which lead her to play the victim or repel men in equal measure.

The kinds of heroines that permanently drive men away are rare creatures. It goes against a prevalent need in our stories to see the heroine come to her senses before she blows it big time. We also like patient heroes, who can offer the undeserving heroine unconditional love. Carrie and Big's ongoing dramas in *Sex and the City* edge around this issue, but in the end the writers make both characters equally responsible. But we still follow Carrie's journey as she works out what she has done. I predict a renaissance in stories in which heroines don't want redemption, don't want reunion, and want to get the hell out. It seems the philosophically minded French are the ones who don't seem to mind their heroines losing it totally. In *Leaving*, the heroine's joyous passion for her lover leads her on an unrepentant path of giving everything up: rich husband, kids, and job. It all has to go. Similarly, in *Villa Amalia*, betrayed Suzanne gives up every aspect of her life she shared with her cheating but repentant long-term partner.

Sometimes an Amazon heroine falls passionately in love with her male Believer counterpart. Their idealism is their primary connection. Together they can change the world! Louise Bryant and John Reed in *Reds*, and Frida Kahlo and Diego Riviera in *Frida*, are of this mode. This kind of love is electric and creative but not particularly stable or family orientated. These couples are a potent force for change, and if they are disillusioned in the other, it's because they think the other is selling out. Infidelity can be borne, so long as their loved one still has their ideals in place.

Darkly loving heroines should be fun to write, and there's not enough of them; deeply sexual women who love on their terms. Lee Holloway in *Secretary* must have given a twist to "first act climax" to the writer. Again it's the French who seem to be setting the standard in sexually exploratory heroines, particularly in the films of Catherine Breillat. If you want to give your heroine a strong interest in her sex life, in a way that doesn't objectify, demean, or romanticize her, there are some useful rules of thumb.

- Number 1: the missionary position is not great for clitoral stimulation.

- Number 2: so much of sex is about talking, touching, and emotion.

- Number 3: the heroine lying back with a blissful expression is just lazy screenwriting.

We still need to see more realistic versions of female desire, including touching and passionate sex scenes from the heroine's point of view. As Nora Ephron showed in *When Harry Met Sally*, faking orgasms is something a woman will do to make her man feel good. Sex doesn't have to be graphic. In *Julie and Julia*, Nora Ephron manages to convey a steamy sexuality in her main characters' relationships by linking their pleasure for good food with impulsive love making! As a writer (particularly if you are a female writer) write sex how you want to see it. And don't fake it!

Rival

Your heroine might set herself up as a Rival to someone else in your story. She might consciously pitch herself against another to prove herself. The role choice of Rival is a galvanizing decision for your heroine, or one that can fuel or reveal her deepest insecurities. Being rivalrous is part of being human and all starts in the family. We are all rivalrous for love, for attention, and to fulfill the needs of our egos. We want to belong, win, and crave recognition for our brilliant selves! For women it is more complex. Much female rivalry originates from many centuries of women being a social minority valued for youth, fertility, and beauty. When it comes to writing your heroine, pay attention to how you develop her as a Rival.

Acceptable clichés abound in stories in which your heroine is a Rival, particularly in comedies. A woman can be as competitive as any man, but it's not seen as such a desirable quality in women. Stories can reveal a monumental sexual double standard here. Men go to war, destroy each other's gangs, and these are glorified. Women have *Bride Wars* and trouble with their *Monster-in-Law*. These films are like battle of the estrogen queens, who finally redeem themselves by seeing the error of their ways at the end. Yawn! *The Devil Wears Prada* explored rivalry between Emily and Andrea with much more comic complexity. Let it set the standard for your comic female-rivalry writing.

The cat fight is the old familiar scenario of two women at each other's throats (metaphorically or otherwise) for the love of the same man. This could be a hangover from the past where marrying well was the best achievement in a woman's life. Having low status equals low self-esteem. Low self-esteem can lead to total indignity, which is often self-imposed. Some women, it's true, would prefer to blame another woman for stealing her man rather than blame the cheat in the first place, like Elle in *Legally Blonde* who believes another woman stole her man rather than face up to the fact that he has dumped her. These women would prefer to beg a man to stay with her even if he's treating her terribly. If it really is your burning goal to have two women pitted against each other in your story, ask yourself *how can I do this in a way that brings something new, is psychologically complex, and isn't too demeaning*?

Sibling Rivalry

Your heroine might be consumed by rivalrous feelings for her sister. Older sisters frequently resent their younger sisters for having it easier, and younger sisters can resent their big sisters for being able to do more in general. *In Her Shoes* follows a dysfunctional relationship between sisters whose mother committed suicide. *A Ma Soeur!* is a warning to all jealous sisters to be careful about what you wish for; if sisterly rivalry interests you then rent it for its shocking denouement. If sibling rivalry is in her backstory, unresolved emotions might play out the way your heroine relates to other women.

Maternal Rivalry

Some mothers can resent their daughters on a deep level. It can be complex because, on the one hand, a mother can identify and almost live through her daughter's experiences, but, on the other hand, her daughter is younger and might have more opportunities than she did. Some mothers are simply threatened by all other women, and that includes their own daughters. Maternal rivalry can make your heroine feel guilty or inadequate, sometimes without really knowing why.

Battle of the Sexes

If your heroine is pitted against a guy or a group of guys in your story, you are letting her join a noble tradition of heroines who battle for equal rights. In *G. I. Jane*, Jordan wants to take on the soldier boys and do it as well if not better.

Tips for Writing the Believer Role Choice

We Are What We Think

When your heroine's ideals and how she sees the world undergo a transformation, the chances are her outer appearance will as well. She will literally become another person. If it's due to love, she might glow and feel and look better. If she's obsessed, she could start losing a grip on her identity.

Sex Scenes

Overt sex scenes are currently out of fashion in mainstream movies, but try to write a sex scene from your heroine's POV. What does she want, feel, and do? How does she express her desires? It's good to know as an exercise in characterization, anyway. Just in case they do come back in fashion!

The Believer Role Choice in Close-Up

Vicky Cristina Barcelona

Vicky and Cristina sit down with Vicky's husband Greg and discuss the threesome relationship Cristina had. Greg is totally shocked, clearly thinking it's unsavoury and unconventional. But Vicky relates to it completely differently, now that she's had the experience of spontaneous passion. Where she was totally judgmental before her own secret one-night stand, she is now open-minded. She isn't at all sure about her values anymore, as her own sense of impending doom about her life as Greg's wife grows.

This scene nicely demonstrates how direct experience of another kind of love has fundamentally changed Vicky's worldview. Her marriage is still viable, but for how long? What kind of Believer is she now?

THE ROLE CHOICE OF CARYATID

A caryatid is a type of column, in the form of a woman, found in the temples of Ancient Greece. It's a good term for heroines who are the institution builders of their worlds — women who support and maintain the status quo. These heroines like order and functionality. You see the Caryatid in your heroine when she's eagerly trying to prove herself on the job by being a loyal wife, running her own business, and generally doing her bit for the establishment.

When she's in this mind-set, your heroine is really the opposite of the role choice of Believer in that she doesn't crave upheaval and transformation. She wants solid foundations and tradition, with the quiet conviction that it's just the right approach. She's a safe pair of hands. This doesn't mean she doesn't fight to conserve or preserve, but her fights will be through established and legal means if necessary.

Contemporary heroines rarely have Caryatid as a dominant role choice in their identity. The Caryatid in a heroine's story is often a supporting character, or even an antagonist. But as a momentary role choice it can give your heroine real backbone when she needs it most. The role choices of Caryatid are Wife, Boss, and Community Pillar.

Wife

The role choice of Wife is one of the most powerfully enduring roles for women. Marriage is an institution that most women don't want to reject, judging by the large numbers of women who get married. Although feminist thought has heavily criticized marriage as an institution, many women today feel they can be married and be equal. Marriage is sacred, special, and the ultimate form of commitment.

The Wife role choice can symbolize a woman's official role in the marriage, which requires a woman to stick to her legal vows and play a part in the fabric of society. In this respect, becoming a wife for your heroine is entering a Caryatid institution, even if she is more of an Amazon at heart. Therefore some heroines' stories revolve around getting out of a marriage gone wrong, or leaving a marriage that she was forced into or that oppresses her somehow. Your heroine might be thought of as a "bad wife" blamed for the relationship breakdown. If she's a Believer like an Amazon, she might be forced into having Caryatid values and can't pull it off. This is a fateful situation. Or she's a Dependant at heart, someone who has a childlike need to be looked after, and who unconsciously relates to her spouse as if he's an overcontrolling parent.

A happily married Amazon heroine will have made a pledge of commitment entirely based on love and devotion. She's a Believer after all. You can be sure that she will be the first to moan about aspects of being married that seriously get on her nerves. And you can be even more certain that her husband will be the first to hear about it!

True Caryatid wives are no nonsense women. They know their roles and responsibilities, and they do their best to meet them. Even sex, even if they don't like it very much. Marriage is a tradition, the normal way of life. Your Caryatid heroine takes her marriage vows very seriously. If she's a Nurturing type too, then she'll be the perfect wife and mother, as far as society goes. Just because she's traditional doesn't mean she can't and doesn't love deeply.

Royal and aristocratic heroines are women who are expected to play their part in society in a Caryatid-like manner. Anne Boleyn in *The Other Boleyn Girl* tries to keep her husband Henry VIII happy but her Amazon and Lover role choices always get in the way. The same applies to Georgiana in *The Duchess*. Georgiana marries when she is very young, not more than a girl, and the grand status of her husband-to-be is exciting to her. Both wives make the big mistake of expecting love to come before duty in a punitive, patriarchal system. A true Caryatid would never make such a mistake. In *Elizabeth*, the young Elizabeth flirts with the idea of love, but she can't hide her true role choice. She's a Caryatid who knows a husband would reduce her ability to rule as she wants. Her decision? To marry England. This is in stark contrast to Victoria in *The Young Victoria*, a different type of Caryatid who discovers she can't handle royal affairs without the support of her husband Albert.

The saddest Caryatids have to be the widows in Deepa Metha's *Water*. They form a rare group of women who are both Caryatids and Victims due to their culture's enforcement of these role choices. Whether young or old, as soon as their husbands die, these women lose all status and have to live far away from their families in the house of widows. Even their heads are shaved, to effectively brand them undesirables.

Boss

A Boss is a woman who has tangible power over others. This role choice is often given to antagonists and secondary characters in stories. Bosses are women who choose to lead, control, and compete rather than nurture. Bosses get a kick out of power and profit, whether it's real or symbolic. They want to achieve, and the domestic sphere is not their favorite place. It's the role choice for your heroine when she is driven, ambitious, and a team leader. Bosses are all about boundaries and sticking to them. They can show "feminine" intuition to do their jobs well, but retaining power and doing the job is the name of the game for these women.

In real life there are many female Bosses, who are wives and mothers. Like Mothers, if a heroine is Boss, the story tends to be about her being a Boss, and, sometimes, the mess she makes of the job. *The Proposal* showed a powerful and bitchy woman, universally hated by her team, who lets down her defenses only after falling in love with her male assistant. In *Mamma Mia!*, Donna's not coping with her rundown hotel. The same goes for motel proprietess Brenda in *Bagdad Café*. For some reason, competent female Bosses in the heroine role aren't as visible on our screens as they are in real life. Our shows are full of women characters in the workplace, however, such as *CSI: Crime Scene Investigation*, *House*, and *Criminal Minds*, to name a few. But the question remains as to why so few women characters are in charge? Does this reflect fear on the producers' part or a reality about women and power? Are women still coming to terms with having power and are anxious about it, unlike men who may have more of an inbuilt sense of entitlement? In the TV show *Damages*, Patty Hewes is a true pioneer as a complex heroine who is a Boss. She has a shifting ethical code, has charismatic character traits, and is brilliant at manipulating others.

Queens

Boss Heroines, when they do exist, are often royals. The heroine's challenge tends to be about attaining or maintaining power, and conflicts in her story tend to revolve around the widespread acceptance of her sex. Queens also lose out on feeling like normal women and are more than acutely aware of what is impermissible in their lives. In *The Queen*, Elizabeth II is not allowed to grieve and nurture her grandsons, nor are her real feelings about Diana, The Princess of Wales, admissible.

Institutional Bosses

There are lots of these in stories, but rarely are they the main character. M in the Bond movies, Pamela Landy in the *Bourne* movies, Corinne in *Rendition*, Miranda in *The Devil Wears Prada*, and Wilhelmina in *Ugly Betty* are all good examples. These women's internal conflicts are kept firmly under control. They are true Caryatids who are motivated to support the institution, but most important to them is their role and status within it.

Evolving Bosses

Weeds explores the criminal rivalry between two women drug dealer bosses, Nancy and Heylia. Both women have families to support and Nurturing role choices to fulfill, yet they crave money and power, and the competition doesn't put them off. Their other role choices can create a great deal of conflict with their role of Boss.

Community Pillar

Community Pillar is the role choice for the female do-gooder. She is all about supporting the community, but unlike a Boss, she doesn't want power. Being a leader is not her style; she prefers to be part of a group. Heroines can choose this role choice when they want to be part of the team or help create something with like-minded others. The emphasis on the role choice is about laying good foundations rather than knocking structures down. Although this role choice doesn't conflict with being family minded, the Community Pillar likes to extend her reach beyond the home.

Crumbling Pillars

Sometimes Community Pillars have a crisis of faith in their values. *Tea with Mussolini* is about a group of Community Pillars in the form of British and American female expatriates in Florence. As Mussolini rises to power, the women's belief in him and their rightful place in Italy are put to the test and eventually shattered. Vera Drake, the illegal abortionist in *Vera Drake*, is a Community Pillar in that she tragically and misguidedly thinks she is only doing good. In both movies, the Community Pillars fall foul of the community and become Outsider Heroines. Community Pillars are frequently found in Sororities, particularly groups of older women. The heroines in *Calendar Girls* and *Ladies in Lavender* function in Sororities. They can be married or are resolute spinsters.

Younger Community Pillars

Gracie Hart in *Miss Congeniality* is an Amazon Community Pillar who has to do good (her police job) by protecting a Sorority of Community Pillars, the beauty queens in peril. Values about femininity clash but ultimately Gracie saves the institution from disruption and danger. Cheerleaders and university sororities in the U.S. and Girl Guides and Brownies in the U.K. are young groups of Community Pillars. Think about what kind of Community Pillar institutions exist for young women in your own culture. What do they stand for?

Tips for Writing the Caryatid Role Choice

Characterizing Cultural Values

Use other characters, even minor ones, to represent the dominant values of the culture your heroine lives in. This doesn't mean endless snippets of dialogue; it can be as simple as an image of a minor character doing something, like walking to church with the family or the community making an effort.

Community Building

If your heroine isn't very traditional, or she's an Outsider, think about ways the status quo might protect or help her. Are there any moments in your story where she has to work to conserve or preserve the status quo despite her distrust in it?

Your Heroine's Identity

Marriage will either make your heroine a stronger person because she's found her soul mate, or it will destroy her sense of identity. Work out how marriage is going to work for her or change her.

The Caryatid Role Choice in Close-Up

An Education

Jenny returns to the girls' school she walked out on to get married before sitting her exams. Now that her relationship is over, she realizes what she has lost. She asks the headmistress if she can come back to school as she has seen the error of her ways. The headmistress is a Boss Caryatid who upholds traditional education for girls. She listens to Jenny but refuses to let her come back. In this short scene, the heroine is tested by the Caryatid who now represents values she finally respects. Through rejection, Jenny becomes even more determined to get to that bastion of the establishment, the University of Oxford.

EXERCISE: YOUR HEROINE'S ROLE CHOICE QUESTIONNAIRE

Imagine you are your heroine as she appears at the start of your story and complete the questionnaire. By the end of the questionnaire you will have developed your heroine's role choices. You will get a better sense of her identity and her relationship to the outside world. As you develop your story, you will be able to see how her role choices might change, as she grows and develops or is put into challenging situations.

YOUR HEROINE'S ROLE CHOICE QUESTIONNAIRE

1. What are your deepest beliefs? What do you stand for?

2. Who or what most influenced these beliefs and ideals?

3. If you have children, how would you describe your parenting style?

4. Who supports you? Do you support others?

5. What does beauty mean to your own identity? Describe your self-image.

6. What do you most love/hate about your job? What would you change about it?

7. If you don't work, why not? How do you support yourself?

8. What are your personal ambitions?

9. What are your career ambitions?

10. How far have you come in achieving them?

11. Describe your position in your community? Do you like your community?

12. How would you like to be remembered?

MAKING IT PERSONAL

Chapter 4

Now that you've got a much clearer idea of your heroine and some of her role choices, it's a good time to start thinking about the meaning of your heroine's story. What is it really about?

FINDING THE STORY

Finding the right story is important to support your theme and what you really want to say by writing your screenplay. What do I mean by story?

A Heroine's Story is her emotional and physical process of experiencing a certain situation that unfolds in a narrative.

You might notice that terms like *solving her problem, following a goal, or coming to terms with so and so* are not at the heart of this definition of story. It's bigger and broader because it encompasses a huge variety of heroines' stories, from U.S. blockbuster to art-house French cinema by way of Japan. Solving problems and having dilemmas are important to certain story types, but very often heroines inhabit stories that go against the grain of conventional dramatic tradition. They might not be about transformation but may be more about exploration of a certain theme or idea. That's why they can be so radical. Some heroine's stories show journeys that end up in a dead-end, with the heroine back where she started. Sometimes heroines don't actually change after their experiences, but the world around them changes. At the risk of repeating myself, a heroine's story is invariably a product of the writer's culture. Not all story traditions are the same. You will know best the story traditions you want to work within and those you want to subvert.

If it helps you, you can think about a heroine's story as her journey, in terms of where your heroine starts from and where she ends up. You might have already thought about a physical journey she might go on, or your story might be more internal and emotional. Or you might be one of those high-concept writers, who always start with an idea you want to play around with.

Working out your heroine story type and theme will help you to develop your heroine's story and bring you closer to what you really want to say.

HEROINE STORY TYPES

A heroine story type is a way of breaking down your heroine's emotional and physical process of her situation (i.e., her story) into a recognizable type. Each heroine story type can be seen as the powerful engine that drives and compels her. All your characters, main and secondary, will have a story type of their own. They do not have to be the same as the heroines, and it is probably better if they aren't.

Heroine story types can work with many different structures, as we will see. They can also appear in any genre of film. It's a good idea to try to choose a story type early, but don't worry if you don't know.

It might be that your heroine distinctly jumps from one heroine story type to another during the course of the film. That's okay! If it makes sense to your story then that's great. But very often, your heroine's story will reflect one dominant story type. Phil Parker, in *The Art and Science of Screenwriting* (1999), defines ten story types; his book is a useful guide for the use of the story types. Here are the main heroine story types that I've identified.

෨෨ Path to Wholeness   ෨෨ Tests of Love
෨෨ Group Endeavor   ෨෨ Quest
෨෨ Survival   ෨෨ The Wandering Woman
෨෨ Rites of Passage   ෨෨ The Talent

Let's have a look at each one.

PATH TO WHOLENESS

The heroine feels emotionally incomplete or wounded; might be completely abused or mentally ill; could be recovering from illness; and might feel totally betrayed or let down by love and she badly needs to recover. Her story focuses on her experience of becoming whole, or trying to become whole. Examples include *I've Loved You So Long*; *Under the Tuscan Sun*; *Boys Don't Cry*; *In Her Shoes*; *Precious*; *Girl, Interrupted*; and *Lost in Translation*.

TESTS OF LOVE

The heroine is absorbed by finding love or experiencing problems in her relationship. Love problems can range from anything as big as war to her own unresolved fear of abandonment (e.g., *When Sally Met Harry*, *Sex and the City: The Movie*). Sweeping epic love stories, such as *The English Patient* and *Cold Mountain*, fall into this type, as do intense dramas such as *The Edge of Love*.

GROUP ENDEAVOR

A group of heroines who depend on each other or live together as a community have an experience together in which they are inter-dependent. It may be a holiday, a quest, or coming to terms with a change from the outside (e.g., *St. Trinian's*, *Female Agents*, *Calendar Girls*, *Tea with Mussolini*, and *The Virgin Suicides*).

QUEST

The heroine gives herself a quest or mission, or is given one by an external factor or person. She spends her time pursuing the quest, even if it ends up having a different outcome than she expected. Quests can range from saving a flock of geese in *Fly Away Home* to finding out the truth about a husband's disappearance in *Rendition* to gaining a law degree at Harvard as in *Legally Blonde*.

SURVIVAL

The heroine's life, or those of the people she loves, is under threat. All her energies revolve around staying alive and outwitting or defeating the forces of destruction. Survival can include emotional survival when the heroine's whole identity is being savaged by another person (e.g., *Elizabeth*, *The Descent*, *Flight Plan*, *The Brave One*, and *Rabbit-Proof Fence*).

WANDERING WOMAN

The heroine needs to keep moving. She's essentially nomadic or naturally an outsider. Her story just might be another stop along the way of her life. She might have found herself stuck and needs to move on but can't. She doesn't feel the need to be whole but her eyes might be opened to other needs as she travels (e.g., the mothers in *Hideous Kinky*, *Chocolat*, *Tumbleweeds*, *Mermaids*, *Alice Doesn't Live Here Anymore*, *TranSylvania*, and *Mona Lisa Smile*).

RITES OF PASSAGE

The heroine is dealing with a major transition that propels her into a new stage of her life. These can be pregnancy, abortion, motherhood, the empty-nest syndrome, stepmotherhood, loss of a child, marriage, divorce, grandmotherhood, and menopause (e.g., *Stepmom*, *10 Things I Hate about You*, and *Thirteen*).

THE TALENT

The heroine has a talent that is central to her sense of identity. In pursuing her talent the heroine encounters many different experiences and obstacles (e.g., *Frida*, *La Vie en Rose*, *Babette's Feast*, *Sylvia*, and *Amelia*).

Choosing a Heroine Story Type

Do any of these grab you? If you are a character-driven writer, you probably can relate to one of these. If you are a concept- or idea-driven writer in the early stages of a story, it might be harder to choose. There's no right or wrong. If you can't decide, you might prefer to think about your theme first. Working out the theme can eventually lead you to find the right heroine story type.

It's very common in the initial stages of writing to think your heroine is on a certain type of story, only to later realize that you really want her focusing on something else. An ensemble screenplay might turn into a single protagonist screenplay, and then you've gone from Group Endeavor to another heroine story type. For instance you might really believe you want to explore the lives of nuns in a convent. One nun keeps shouting for your attention, and before you know it, you're giving her a great deal more narrative space. Depending on what the nun is bothered about, you can find her individual heroine story type. If she's having a crisis of faith, she's probably following the Path of Wholeness. If she's fallen in love with the convent gardener, she's on a Test of Love heroine story type. If it's a horror film, and the devil has infiltrated the convent, then suddenly she's following the Survival heroine story type.

If you really can't decide, ask your heroine! Sit down and write a stream of consciousness from her point of view. Remember how she persuaded you to give her the role of heroine in the first place?

Heroines Story Types in Close-Up

In *4 Months, 3 Weeks and 2 Days*, Otilia is on a quest to support Gabi's effort to have an illegal abortion. Her quest involves some horrible twists and turns, in which she will be forced to sleep with the bullying and misogynistic abortionist and risk years of imprisonment in Romania. Gabi is on a rites of passage story as she experiences the decision to get rid of her baby. She is vulnerable, passive, and frightened.

Mona Lisa Smile has a Wandering Woman heroine story type. Katherine Ann finds herself, for a while, at Wellesley College, a fish out of water as wandering women so often are. The dramatic question is will she stay at Wellesley? Her free-spirited thinking clashes with the conservative and reactionary values of the Wellesley culture. The different girls who are taught by her all have different heroine story types. By the end, Katherine Ann moves on.

In *A Ma Soeur!* Anais is on the Path to Wholeness. She is consumed by her confusing feelings about sibling rivalry and her lowly position in the family for being the fat and ugly daughter. Her sister follows the heroine story type of Tests of Love, as her boyfriend sleeps with her and forces her to have anal sex. Anais' fantasizes about love and escape from her family, and finally her unconscious wishes are brought to life in a terrible way.

THEME

I'm one of those writers who might start out thinking that I have a theme, but who finds out further down the line that another theme feels more relevant to what's going on in the story. I don't think you can rush your themes. I think, like cream, they rise to the top with every story document you produce in the early stages of developing your idea. Finally you click. You realize what your story is really about. If you try and find your theme too early, you can put yourself under unnecessary pressure.

What Is a Theme?

Well, the jury is out on this subject, and the definitions in screen-writing guides can be fairly diverse. For the purposes of writing your heroine's story, here is mine.

A theme is the underlying message behind your story.

It's pretty simple. It's your argument, really. It's the secret message you want to whisper in the ears of your audience so that when they leave the movie theater or the living room they think your philosophical viewpoint was their idea!

Your theme's main job is audience satisfaction. No one likes being preached at, so you have to bury it. It has to become a subliminal message, at least for the vast majority of your screenplay. Everyone likes a profound moment of enlightenment about the human condition, even if in a fluffy comedy. So you do have to find your theme.

Finding Your Theme

When I say don't rush it, I don't mean forget about it and wait for it to pop up. You have to do some work for the cream to rise. You have to make sure the cow is properly fed and milked in the first place! Your job is to work on your character and story in a simultaneous process in the early stages of development. Every writer develops their own processes. Here is how mine goes.

- I get an idea about my character.

- I have a strong idea of a concept and the kind of story type I think my heroine will lead.

- I do a great deal of character work, trying to find out who my heroine is. I do the exercises I've shared with you.

- I start to research my heroine's world. If she's a real character, the biographies come out. Google becomes my best friend. I trot to the local university library and surround myself in dusty tomes. I write a huge amount of notes.

- I consult the screenwriting books of my favorite gurus! A story starts to form, with secondary characters and sources of conflict. A story type takes on a strong level of appeal.

- I sketch out story lines in the form of beat sheets. Loads of them! On the train, while I'm doing the dishes, in the shower, the creative back burner starts to swing into action. I panic when I can't find a pen in my bag, or that scrap of cardboard I wrote something totally essential on. I become difficult to live with!

- Many versions end up in the bin. I realize my character needs to change in some areas, and some story ideas don't make so much sense. The whole concept of what I want this story to say starts to change.

- Secondary characters and sources of conflict become redefined.

Then all of a sudden, I have a lightbulb moment! I suddenly realize *what I really want to say.*

Whatever your process, it takes some work to find your theme. Even if you have one at the beginning, be open to change. If don't have one, but have a vague idea, for example, *love and hate in an artists' community*, then do the development work, and the real theme will come.

When it does, it will be more specific and have a slant, such as "art can be destroyed by those who treasure it most." It should feel like Robert Mckee's Controlling Idea in *Story* (1999), which is a good great guide to theme. Your theme is a golden and priceless product of an alchemical process involving your unconscious, creativity, and story-telling talent. It probably reflects what you stand for as a person. I don't believe you can ever really pick your theme totally consciously, but you can refine it once you've found it.

Writing with Your Theme

Your ultimate challenge, when you do get around to writing the first draft of your screenplay, is to make sure that your theme is as deeply buried as possible in the first ten pages. This is widely accepted good practice in the screenwriting business. Many experts think you can see the whole story, metaphorically and symbolically, in the first ten pages. I agree.

Remember, themes work best when they are subliminal. Your audience will be so caught up with your heroine and her M-Factor, problems, and world that they won't be actively looking for it anyway (unless they are screenwriters, who if they are anything like me, are the biggest pains to watch films with!). All the same, it has to be there, working its magic.

Every character and scene will then reflect your theme. As you write, you might feel tested by trying to keep it buried, but you will manage it. Further drafts will then start to feel tighter. You will sense the essential "truth" of your story emerging, stronger and clearer, with each draft. The cream has risen to the top!

You will finally, by the third act, be able to let a character even articulate the theme, from her own viewpoint. Take the artists' community. Your heroine artist might be contemplating her great painting when she realizes how much she misses her lover from the artist's community. But while she loved him, her work lacked focus, and her sales dried up. So in Act 3, she just might say "I miss him." But the audience will know she's evaluating exactly what this priceless masterpiece has cost her personally. Was it worth it? But while she was with him, love came first. Wait until the third act for this kind of direct revelation.

There is however, another way to find the theme. I'm telling you about this later because I didn't want to deprive you of your lightbulb moment, which is one of the great pleasures of creativity. But this other way might satisfy you more, it depends on the kind of writer you are. This other way is by finding your story's Metaphoric Wound.

THE METAPHORIC WOUND

All heroines, like all humans, carry around deeply buried unresolved pain. If she is lucky, your heroine will heal this pain during the course of her story. If she isn't so lucky, the story will function to explore her pain rather than resolve it. You might be wondering about those heroines who are fully functional human beings until something terrible happens? Well, first you have to be honest and ask yourself if there really are people with absolutely no emotional scars or buried pain? Obviously not. But it is possible that your story is about the worse thing to happen to your heroine so far in her life.

The deepest and most buried pain of your heroine symbolizes something I call the Metaphoric Wound of your story. In powerful stories, this deeply buried pain can be seen in many layers of your heroine's life and world. The Metaphoric Wound is the deepest layer of meaning in your story, even deeper than the theme. Once you find out what your Metaphoric Wound is, it can help you find your theme. I will show you how to do this, but first let's find out more about the Metaphoric Wound.

The Metaphoric Wound is the deepest pain experienced by your heroine that is metaphorically visible in the wider world of her story.

The Metaphoric Wound can be seen in the following levels of your heroine's world:

The Wider Culture

The Metaphoric Wound can be seen in the values and customs of the wider world and will have an impact on the community.

The Community

The Metaphoric Wound can function in the way your heroine's community is organized, and how people within the community treat each other. In turn, it can affect the family.

The Family

The Metaphoric Wound is often generated here, and it can be seen in how the family functions as a group. Your heroine can be wounded by her experiences here.

The Individual

The Metaphoric Wound caused by the family or a family member will have particular effect on your heroine and will represent her deepest pain.

Finding the Metaphoric Wound

To find the Metaphoric Wound, you have to delve into your heroine's backstory, and then you have to look at the "here and now" of her world in the story. The things you are looking for are her Internal Wound, Internal Gift, External Gift, and External Wound. What do I mean by these?

Internal Wound

This is the most deeply felt emotional pain that your heroine has ever experienced. For a great deal of people, this is caused in childhood by a parental figure, or it is any severely traumatic event. You have to work out what this is for your heroine by looking deep into her past and present. It may be buried and deeply repressed but comes out in how she functions in relation to herself and other people. Your story might tell the cause of her Internal Wound, and what happens next, just like Lily in *The Secret Life of Bees*.

Internal Gift

Your heroine's Internal Gift is the best coping mechanism that she has developed to protect herself from internal pain and conflict. You can see it as a defense mechanism in her psychology. It doesn't have to actually be very positive. A self-harmer might find the experience of cutting herself a release, like Lee in *Secretary*. This is her coping mechanism, her internal gift. You might think that *gift* is not really the right word, but I think it fits the bill because it reflects the high value your heroine unconsciously places on this defense mechanism.

External Gift

Now move away from the backstory and into the here and now of your heroine's world in your story. Ask yourself what in her story is potentially the best thing that could happen to her and is a real possibility? What could bring her the most happiness? If she can accept the External Gift, emotionally, and be open to it, she will get a great deal of happiness from it. The External Gift is so powerful that it can solve your heroine's problems.

External Wound

Staying in the story, ask yourself what your heroine thinks is her biggest problem right now. You might want to look at this as the biggest obstacle she has to solve, or simply the thing in her life that causes her the most sleepless nights.

Okay, so you think you've got these? If you aren't quite sure, don't worry because we will go through some film examples. But first, I want you to absorb the following Metaphoric Wound governing principles.

The Metaphoric Wound Governing Principles

1. Your heroine's Internal Gift, her coping mechanism, feeds the External Wound.

2. The Internal Gift is a paradox. It helps your heroine cope, but it gets in the way of her solving her actual problem.

3. The External Wound is fed by the unresolved Internal Wound. Your heroine's lack of resolution means that she is somehow, consciously or unconsciously, contributing to her own problem.

4. The Internal Gift has to be given up or sacrificed to achieve the External Gift.

5. Healing the Internal Wound achieves the External Gift.

6. The Metaphoric Wound of your story is your heroine's Internal

Wound seen thematically. It is visible in all those layers I described previously.

7. The Metaphoric Wound is not necessarily healed in the story. If you, the writer, remain unconscious of the Wound, you might not resolve it. Similarly, you might decide that your character, for whatever reason, is unable to heal themselves. It might support your theme to convey a bleak message.

I know it seems complicated, which is why we're going to look at some film examples to see how it all works.

The Metaphoric Wound in a Heroine's Story

All About My Mother

Manuela is the heroine. She is a donor transplant administrator, whose son Walter is killed in front of her eyes, while he chases an actress for her autograph. Manuela's Internal Wound is the loss of her only son. Walter's death triggers memories of Manuela's previous loss, of her husband and Walter's father, when she was pregnant eighteen years earlier. He didn't die, but she left him when he became a transsexual "Lola."

Manuela's Internal Gift is running away, her coping mechanism. She has been running away from Lola for eighteen years and never told Walter who his father was. Her External Wound is the fact that she has to face her ex-husband Lola again. This is because she wants to honor Walter, because just before he was killed, Manuela promised she would tell him who his father was.

Manuela's External Gift is finally moving on, and with a new chance at motherhood. She is given a new baby to look after, also called Walter and fathered by Lola. Lola impregnated Rosa, but as he had AIDS he also gave her the virus. When Rosa dies, she leaves Walter in Manuela's care, because Manuela cared for Rosa during her illness and became her surrogate mother. Now let's see how the Metaphoric Wound principles relate.

Manuela's Internal Gift, running away, feeds the External Wound, which is not facing Lola and her guilty feelings over not telling Walter who his father was. Her Internal Wound, loss of Walter, feeds her External Wound, facing Lola. But if she doesn't face Lola, her pain over Walter will continue. She has to relinquish her Internal Gift, running away, by going back to face Lola to honor Walter. If she tells Lola of Walter's existence, then in some small way she will have kept her promise to Walter. By relinquishing her Internal Gift, her coping mechanism of running away, Manuela is led to Rosa and eventually finds her External Gift, Rosa's baby, for whom she becomes a mother again.

The Metaphoric Wound in *All About My Mother* is Loss. This directly evolves from the heroine's own Internal Wound of loss, as we have seen. Now let's see how the Metaphoric Wound is evident on all levels of Manuela's world, from her wider culture down to her own sense of identity.

Wider Culture: The AIDS epidemic provides the backdrop, meaning widespread loss of life.

Community: Manuela works in donor transplants, which depend on the loss of someone's life. In Barcelona she works for an actress, Huma, who was accidentally responsible for her son's death, and who plays in *Street Car Named Desire*, which is all about loss of love, sanity, friendship.

Family: Manuela has lost her son. She also loses Rosa, who has become a surrogate daughter to her. Agrada has lost her best friend Lola. Rosa's mother loses her daughter. Huma loses her lover. Rosa's father has lost his mind. All these characters that constitute Manuela's "family" lose somebody.

Identity: Manuela loses the meaning of her life when she loses Walter.

The Metaphoric Wound is healed by the renewal of life. This links to the theme of *All About My Mother*, which could be described as "people can renew if they face their losses." Manuela, as heroine, could have sunk into despair after Walter's death. Instead, she seeks closure and in doing so heals her Internal Wound. As you can see, every character and every scene of *All About My Mother* reflects the theme of loss somehow. Now let's see the Metaphoric Wound in a very different movie with two Heroines.

The Holiday

Strangers to each other, British Iris and American Amanda are both hurt by love and decide to house-swap for the holidays. They enter each other's worlds. Amanda describes her own Internal Wound when she tells Graham, her British lover, that the most painful things in her life were her parent's breakup and the loss of her father.

Iris' Internal Wound is harder to find, but there are clues in the story. She's in love with Jasper who uses her shamelessly, yet she forgives him every time. When we learn that Iris' mother is a publishing executive, you can't help but think there was a problem in the mother/daughter relationship for Iris to have such low self-esteem. But that is her Internal Wound — desperately low self-esteem. Amanda's External Wound is messing up another relationship when she really wants one to work. For Iris, it's Jasper's engagement to another woman when she is still in love with him.

As for the two heroines' Internal Gifts, for Amanda is it not being able to cry. She is so well defended against pain she can't let feelings overwhelm her even if she tries. Her crying capacity is in lockdown. For Iris, it is putting other people's needs before her own and being utterly dependable, even to the point of masochism. Their External Gifts are again different; for Amanda, it comes in the form of a devoted and warm man, Graham. For Iris, it's learning to be the leading lady in her own life.

Amanda's self-protection has fed her External Wound of dysfunctional relationships with men. She has to give up her Internal Gift of self-protection by allowing herself to feel for Graham, her External Gift. This happens when she leaves Graham, whose love has touched her. By healing her Internal Wound and opening up to be vulnerable, she achieves her External Gift, a really good relationship and no more loneliness.

For Iris, it's a little different. Her Internal Wound of inadequacy creates her External Wound of a masochistic relationship, which leaves her lonely. Her Internal Gift of dependability feeds her problems with Jasper, her External Wound. By giving up dependability in order to look after herself better, she is finally able to let go to receive her External Gift of "gumption" — being the leading lady of her life. This brings her to the healthier promise of a relationship with Miles.

The Metaphoric Wound in *The Holiday* is loneliness. In stories with two or more main characters, see what their Internal Wounds have in common. In *The Holiday*, Iris' low self-esteem and Amanda's steely emotional defenses keep them both single and alone. Now let's see how the Metaphoric Wound, loneliness, is evident on all levels of Amanda and Iris' worlds, from the wider culture down to their own sense of identity.

Wider Culture: It's a culture where thirty-something women are trying to find love, and it's not easy!

Community: Amanda's community is driven and workaholic Hollywood where it is easy to let work take over your life. Iris works as a newspaper wedding columnist, reminding herself on a daily basis of her single status.

Family: Iris' brother Graham has lost his wife and is clearly lonely. His family group is sad and lonely. Amanda suffers the loneliness of her own broken family. Elderly Arthur who Iris helps is a lonely widower.

Identity: Iris's and Amanda's problems result in them both being alone for the holidays and, potentially, single women throughout their lives.

The Metaphoric Wound of loneliness is healed by both heroines facing their emotional issues. This links to the theme of *The Holiday*, which could be described as "loneliness ends when you deal with your issues." Iris could have continued being controlled by Jasper, but the guidance of Arthur and a new friend in Miles helps her move on. Amanda could have continued to throw herself into work and continue a string of bad affairs, but Graham and his daughters show her how to be brave and open up.

The Metaphoric Wound and Theme

In both films you can see that the Metaphoric Wound, stemming from the heroines' deepest inner conflicts, is reflected in all levels of the story's world. I've shown how the theme is your particular philosophical interpretation of the Metaphoric Wound. Your story, including every character and every scene, should reflect an aspect of your theme. Remember the Metaphoric Wound is only one way of finding your theme. We all have our own processes. You might be a writer for whom a certain theme is your very first motivating factor to write the story.

Back to the Story Type

Now that you've thought through your Metaphoric Wound and your theme, go back and take another look at the heroine story types. You've done a great deal of thinking about what is going on for your heroine on a deep level, so one of the story types might feel a great deal more resonant for you.

∽ In *All About My Mother*, Manuela is on a Path to Wholeness heroine story type.

∽ In *The Holiday*, Amanda and Iris are also on a Path to Wholeness heroine story type.

This is the heroine story type when the female character is stuck in her life because of internal issues. The story makes her deal with these.

Tips for Writing the Metaphoric Wound

Don't Panic!

If you can't work out what the Metaphoric Wound is at first, remain calm. The more you work on your heroine's internal conflicts, the more you will be able to find it.

Be Brave... and Honest!

Your story and its theme are always going to be deeply influenced by your own philosophies about life, which are drawn from your own life experiences. If you can think about your own Internal Wounds and Gifts, you might be able to see the Metaphoric Wound in your own life. We all have them, and we usually get a sense of them when we come up against the same patterns in life and relationships. If you don't heal them, they can reflect in the stories you are choosing to write. You could say that we writers write best that which we need to heal.

The funny thing is, when you've resolved certain conflicts in your own life, your story choices tend to change. If you can see this happening, this is truly conscious screenwriting. Another good thing to do is watch movies: try to work out the Wounds and Gifts of the main character. Also try to see what heroine story type they might be following.

Minor Characters

Remember they have an important function, which is to reflect your theme and that alone. If they aren't doing that, then either cut them or help them become more relevant.

EXERCISE: YOUR HEROINE'S GIFTS AND WOUNDS QUESTIONNAIRE

To get you started, complete Your Heroine's Gifts and Wounds questionnaire, again from your heroine's point of view. If you want to work on your conscious screenwriting, then you could always fill it out from your point of view too!

YOUR HEROINE'S GIFTS AND WOUNDS QUESTIONNAIRE

1. What is the worst thing that has ever happened to you?

2. How does it make you feel now?

3. How do you cope with it?

4. Are there any people in your life who make you feel bad about yourself? Why?

5. How do you behave when you are around people who make you feel bad about yourself?

6. How would you like to change your behavior toward them?

7. How do you make yourself feel good?

8. Who makes you feel good about yourself?

9. What kind of relationship would you like to develop with people who make you feel good?

10. If you could make a wish, what would it be?

A PHASE
SHE'S GOING THROUGH

It's now time to focus on building your heroine's story. I'd like to introduce you to the concept of the phase as a building block of the story type. By using phases you will also be able to develop your character and theme and support your structure.

A phase is a moment or duration of time in the story when your heroine has experiences or makes decisions that affect her identity.

Phases are a new way of looking at stories and how to build them. Because they are related to your heroine's identity, they explore what she is doing in the story at any given moment. The best way of describing them is the substance of identity. They basically deal with your character's subjectivity throughout the story. That's why they can come in any order you like.

It might help to think of a phase like the phase of the moon, which transmits a different energy. In the same way, a phase in your heroine's journey is a moment or duration of narrative time with a particular energy. A phase is not a stage, because they don't have to go in any order.

How *you* as a writer experience each phase is shaped by the Superthemes influencing you, your heroine's character and role choices at any given moment, the heroine story type you've chosen, and the theme and Metaphoric Wound you are exploring. Phases can bring a great deal together. Ultimately, how your heroine will experience each phase is shaped by her unique character. She might be identifying with a certain role choice, but a phase will show how she's relating to it, when she is, and what she does with it. You'll see this as you get to know each phase. The phases can be categorized in three groups:

IDENTITY PHASES	RELATING PHASES	MOMENTUM PHASES
∾ Transition	∾ Self-Relegation	∾ Violation
∾ Maternal Lessons	∾ Desire for Union	∾ Crossroads
∾ Father Distance	∾ Loving Too Much	∾ Eruption
∾ Adornment	∾ Retreat	∾ Path to Potential

THE PHASES AND THEME

Thinking through each phase and its effect on your heroine can help you develop your theme better. This is because phases ask you to question your stance on certain issues. Phases deal with your heroine's identity and the many choices she will make as a girl or a woman. These can include sexuality, gender issues, motherhood, marriage and divorce, work, loss, aging, relationships, and the female body. You'll be having insights about these areas that feel real for your heroine, and these might inspire your story's theme.

For instance, in *Sex and the City: The Movie*, Carrie spends a long time in the Retreat phase. During this time, she is able to work out her contribution to her and Big's disastrous wedding, which reflects the theme of the film. I believe the theme of *Sex and the City: The Movie* is something along the lines of "True love requires self-truth." All the characters in the film have to deal with their denial of what they are do-ing wrong, which is damaging either their relationships or their identity. For heroine Carrie, she needs to work it out in the Retreat phase, which I will describe a bit later.

A phase energizes the story and takes on a unique form because of several unique factors that only you control. These factors are your heroine's personality, emotional wounds, culture, and opportunities and challenges. As you get to know each phase, use them to inspire your own interpretation of how your heroine might relate to them and decide where in the story they might work. You will also be able to increasingly recognize them in films and shows that you watch.

PHASES AND STRUCTURE

The phases are truly flexible, and there's absolutely no prescriptive ways when it comes to using them. Each heroine's story reflects them in completely different ways. They are not blueprints for structure. Phases complement any structure of screenplay you use, whether it's the classic linear structure, a "complex" linear structure (where the narrative unfolds in two or three different linear story lines), an art-house nonlinear structure, or even a circular structure.

I can't really emphasize their flexibility enough. First imagine your structure as the loom. Then imagine the phases as strands of thread that weave through your screenplay. Just as in a tapestry, certain colors of thread will be stronger in certain sections and weaker in others. The colors might disappear for a while, only to come back later. Some threads you can see in the background running evenly all the way through. Some phases just might not feel right for your story. They might work better as aids to help you develop the backstory of your heroine (all her life experience until the story begins).

Now let's look at each group of phases in more detail. You can use them to help you structure your story by mapping which phases feel right for each act. But as you get to know and use them, you'll find that they become alive.

THE IDENTITY PHASES

The Identity phases reflect the moments in the story that are concerned with your heroine's *changing* identity. It's where she's dealing with her direction in life, the things getting in the way of finding herself, and the image she presents to herself and the world.

The Identity Phases are Transition, Maternal Lessons, Father Distance, and Adornment:

∞ The Transition phase reflects your heroine's initiation of change in her story.

∾ The Maternal Lessons phase shows your heroine dealing with her values about being a woman.

∾ The Father Distance phase shows your heroine dealing with issues about men and masculinity.

∾ The Adornment phase concerns your heroine relating to her own physical being and self-esteem issues.

Transition

All heroines want a change, even if this need is not consciously recognized by them. Changes can be chosen, enforced, or even coincidental. It can be brought on by one of women's many physical changes through life, menstruation, ovulation, pregnancy, birth, menopause, and aging. In your story, the Transition phase is when your heroine is in freefall having taken the plunge, whether she is pushed or she jumped. It is the period of time when she endures the loss of the old and anticipates the new. It signifies a fundamental change of direction.

On a psychological level, your heroine may be ready for change or totally unprepared for it. Or she could be somewhere in between the two, of two minds and hesitant. A heroine may be feeling confident, vulnerable, or even terrified at the unknown quantity of the prospects ahead. In the Transition phase, a heroine tends to be out of her depth, but there is absolutely no going back. Your heroine may have walked out on a marriage, started a new job, decided to commit suicide, or got pregnant. There is a general feeling of release in this stage, like a leap of faith. The point is your heroine is on the verge of a new life, which will change her in a way she doesn't yet know.

Your heroine may start her journey in Transition at the beginning of your story, similar to so many heroines in films. In *Mona Lisa Smile*, Katharine Ann arrives at Wellesley College not knowing what to expect but she's full of motivation. Alternatively, Transition might occur much farther along in her journey, or even at the end. It can also reoccur several times during the course of your narrative, at any point she has to move on and out.

Sometimes water can literally symbolize Transition on a heroine's journey. In *Villa Amalia*, the heroine drifts in the sea, not moving or drowning, until she is saved by a young Italian couple. *The Piano* uses the sea to symbolize transition in the emotional life of heroine Ada. Water is the replenishing source of life, but it can take life away just as easily. Like Ada, your heroine might have to make the choice to sink or swim at this point in her journey.

Maternal Lessons

Every woman "deals" with being a woman every day of her life, whether this is conscious or unconscious. All women have issues about being a woman — angry, happy, contented, frustrated, and complicated; you name it, your heroine will have experienced it at some point in her life. Your heroine might not even be aware of some of the baggage about her sex and gender that she might be carrying around. She might be totally unconscious of a deep underlying rage with men. She might completely identify with men and shun any conventional notions of femininity, or be a tomboy, butch lesbian, or transvestite.

Maternal Lessons represent the mother/daughter relationship. As women in Western culture mainly do the lion's share of the child-drearing, the mother is normally the first relationship for a baby. The mother looms large in a baby's early life, an omnipotent force. She is a goddess-like being on which her daughter is completely dependent for survival. Some adult women feel they cannot ever achieve distance from their mother, no matter what they do. Where a boy can more easily separate from his mother because he has a male father and masculine culture to welcome him, the girl has to accept that she will become like her mother, who she is trying to individuate from. You can see this seemingly unbreakable bond in mother-daughter relationships, even the bad ones.

A mother is a girl's strongest and most powerful role model, who wittingly or unwittingly transmits powerful messages about being female. Your heroine lives those messages, either by rejecting them or embracing them. If your heroine is a mother, she will be giving her own maternal lessons to her children. Many women consciously do everything possible to not turn into their mothers. But if your heroine has a close and loving relationship to her mother, it will be harder for her to resist identification with her mothers' values, whatever they are. This can include resentment of the father in the family. Mothers, because they do so much of the nurturing, tend to set the standard for emotional literacy in the family. If a mother is immature, then her daughter's struggles to express herself will be harder.

Power Corrupts

By the very nature of the role of mother, women have a great deal of power in the family. For some women, it's the only place they do have power. The family unit is her territory and her property, and she can defend this and wage war for the rest of her life. This can lead to the high sense of betrayal and abandonment issues women feel after a divorce, even if they sought the divorce. It can also make women feel their ex is still their property, despite *decree absolute*.

So how do Maternal Lessons function as a phase in your story? They pretty much boil down to one premise: what being a woman means to your heroine. What if she didn't have a mother? Well, that's a lesson in itself, one all about loss. Unhelpful lessons that your heroine might believe can take this form:

∞ Women's lives are hard.

∞ Women should be looked after by men.

∞ Women should put their needs second and put others first.

∞ Women are rivals to each other for male attention.

∞ Women shouldn't trust men.

∞ Women have to be beautiful to get ahead.

∞ Don't explore your body.

∞ If you eat that you'll get fat.

∞ If you form a relationship with your father's new partner you are being disloyal to me.

∞ Women should stick together.

∞ Keep young and beautiful.

Although helpful lessons can look like this:

- Women can be independent.

- Women have a right to childcare.

- Men can be as good a parent as a woman.

- Women's aging processes are beautiful.

- This is what you should understand about your body....

- Women should be clear about all their needs, emotional, sexual, professional, and so forth.

- Women have a right to earn the same as men.

- You are going to have a happy and fulfilling life!

Over the course of your heroine's story, she will gradually arrive at a point where these lessons can be challenged in some way. She will abandon them, defend them, or at the very least have a major rethink. This phase will appear in your screenplay, when a heroine is confronted with or acts out her internalized values about being a woman, whether she's doing it consciously or unconsciously. Very often, by the end, she will unlearn them. Check out the three heroine/daughters in French film *L'enfer* (Hell) whose whole lives have been damaged by the irrational campaign of hate that their mother has for their father (who turns out to be not so bad after all).

Self-Image

In *The Devil Wears Prada* Andrea starts her journey not particularly image conscious and with a bunch of good friends, male and female. Her encounter with fashion guru Miranda forces her to adopt the nasty values of high fashion where women are cold and ruthless, showing little support to each other. Some heroines have an inner rivalry with other women. She's the compulsive perfectionist who always looks good, the kind of woman who can bring out a sense of inferiority in other women. Scarlett O'Hara is queen of this tribe. Carrie Bradshaw comes a close second in the style department, but her outer fashion confidence partly masks her inner insecurities. Elle in *Legally Blonde* has helpful and unhelpful Maternal Lessons. Utterly superficial and defined by her looks, Elle has a loving mom who is a little shallow. But deep down, Elle trusts women. Elle's Maternal Lessons come in the form of entitlement for being blonde and beautiful. She's been taught Maternal Lessons such as women are her friends and women should look good to land an Alpha-male husband. These lessons form a powerful phase in the first half of the film but are quickly unlearned later at Harvard.

Sometimes a heroine just can't relate to men because her mother has instilled that the male sex is dangerous and threatening. The mother in Peruvian film *The Milk of Sorrow* teaches her daughter that men are brutally dangerous, will rape her, and must be avoided. Some heroines believe it's a women's versus men world, and that women should stick together for protection. German film *A Question of Silence* is another great example.

Father Distance

A father is probably your heroine's first hero. What do I mean by hero? Well, in the case of a girl child her father is normally the first person who can help her loosen the bond and dependency on her mother. This might be stating the obvious but in your heroine's life, her attitude toward men will be shaped by that first relationship. If your heroine has a father who provided all the nurturing warmth, intimacy, and care that a mother is expected to, then she probably is pretty balanced about men and women. She's got a solid foundation of self-esteem that has been validated by the love she had from both parents. But many women's experiences with fathers, however loving, are that they aren't so available, are busy, work, or simply didn't live in the family. Or women have absolutely no notion who their fathers are. Worse-case scenario, fathers are abusive, sexually, physically, or emotionally. Equally damaging is when a girl has Maternal Lessons that tell her men are bad in some way.

All these can amount to girls sometimes feeling a kind of Father Distance. This can create a sense of hunger, dissatisfaction, or insecurity in your young heroine about men. She will show these feelings in different ways because every woman's childhood is different, but they can manifest in a need to seek approval from men. The woman will have anger with men, low self-esteem, feelings of inner emptiness, fear of abandonment, and be prone to losing a sense of identity by looking after other people. A heroine might internalize some messages, like these:

- You will accept that you will be judged and defined for your looks.

- You will not grow old, and if you do, you will try to hide it for as long as possible.

- You will be the main caretaker of children.

- You will learn to put your own needs second.

- You will dread being called slut and modify your sexual behavior accordingly.

- You will feel inhibited about asking for what you really want in bed.

- The family come before your career.

- If you want your marriage to work, you will put your career second.

Obviously, no man speaks like this, and many women certainly feel they live life on their own terms and with supportive men. But watching some films from world cinema, it is very clear that these messages still permeate women's lives. These are the worst aspects of ways of being that keep women back. Even in the postfeminist West, sexist and subliminal messages can persist. This is what the Father Distance phase is all about, those moments or periods of time in the story when your heroine has issues with men because of masculine expectations. Let's see how the Father Distance phase plays itself out in some movies.

What does Bridget Jones verbally beat herself up for? Being fat and unsophisticated. She's not so worried about the one thing she probably should worry about — her neurotic low self-esteem and desperation to marry. Mark Darcy is the ultimate romantic hero. Like a tolerant father he indulges, overlooks, and generally gets a kick out of his blonde bubble of naïveté. Even in the sequel, *Bridget Jones: The Edge of Reason*, patient Mark withstands all Bridget's infantile testing. When you look at Bridget's bumbling father and limited mother, you understand why she idolizes Mark for his extremely manly competence.

Some films focus on women getting over the scars of Father Distance. *Volver* shows Raimunda coming to terms with the fact that Father Distance in the culture has left her working full time, cooking and cleaning for a male slob who tries to rape her daughter. Later Raimunda's own childhood abuse by her father is revealed. In *Vicky Cristina Barcelona*, Vicky's upscale fiancé promises a stability that is all about conventional roles. Ultimately, the promise of wealthy Manhattan marriage wins out over a high-octane fling with no guarantees. And free spirit Cristina? She realizes that whatever passion she finds with a man or woman (or both), it soon deflates back into the mundane.

Father Distance is the principle behind the creation of every sensitive romantic hero, and every two-timing cheat. As a phase in your heroine's story, Father Distance reflects a heroine projecting her deepest feelings about men onto another character, usually male. Sometimes, the Father Distance phase isn't very romantic after all. That's because it isn't about real love at all, it's about your heroine's unresolved projections about men.

On the positive side, many heroines don't have any negative idea of Father Distance because they have loving and close relationships with their fathers, even if they don't live with them. Andrea in *The Devil Wears Prada* has an emotionally supportive father and an absent mother. Her issues with mother figures are highlighted when she gains a ruthless female boss. For these heroines, Father Distance will only affect them in their external lives, for instance, if there is a glass ceiling at work.

Many Fighting Femininity films weave in the Father Distance phase throughout the whole narrative. *The Circle* follows a group of women coping with the oppressive sexist society in Iran. Remember Josie Aimes taking out a class action suit about sexual harassment in the mining industry?

Self-limiting attitudes prevent your heroine from real emotional growth. Think about the characters in your story that represent her internal conflicts and projections. Who is going to help her solve her attitudes? Do you want her ideas about men to change over the course of the narrative or do you want the male-dominated world to change for your heroine?

Adornment

The huge emphasis on women's looks affects all women, and it will also affect your heroine one way or another. Very often, her attitude to her self-image is given to your heroine in the form of a Maternal Lesson and Father Distance. How much you acknowledge this in your story is up to you, but it is a reality in all women's lives. Far more than men ever will be, a woman is judged by her looks first and her brains second. We are all so conditioned to do this, it's almost instinctive. Fiona in *Shrek* is a positive role model to us all for accepting how we look!

You might notice that the first time you describe your heroine you have to stop yourself from defining her level of attractiveness. I do it all the time, and I have to question myself. Am I trying to appeal to a certain actress? Am I making my heroine more acceptable to others? It's a familiar scenario, and one I've trained myself out of. Now I write her dominant attitude first. If I do describe looks, I try to avoid words such as *attractive* or *beautiful* because it isn't how I'd describe a male character, at least not in the first instance.

Our culture is hooked on female beauty. It's very hard not to feel the pressure to look good. Not making an effort is seen as not doing your best. But why? What are we so scared of? As writers, can we be more imaginative with how concepts such as beauty and looking good affect our heroine? Maybe these questions clash with your own attitudes about image. Maybe you just think looking as good as possible is the right thing to do.

The need to adorn is driven into women at younger and younger ages. Female attractiveness is a currency that young women quickly realize they are rich in, if not they better develop some other assets. The premium on women's beauty is a hangover from less equal times, but it still can govern our daily lives and sense of identity. It's why girls as young as six are getting anorexia and women as young as thirty are having brow lifts. It's easy to forget that many girls — even most —

have to get over difficult rites of passage during which they learn they are objects for general visual consumption. The girl has three choices: to collude with expectations of femininity, reject them, or somehow fudge the deal for some self-respect. Some teenage girls find the transition to being on the receiving end of objectification so painful, they hate their bodies and want to conceal them. The end result is a great deal of ambivalence and anxiety about their image that women learn to accept. The bottom line that our culture ignores is that it is undignified to be assessed and valued for your market rate in the looks department. We've forgotten feeling humiliated is a logical response to being objectified. We mask it by pretending it's normal to define oneself by other people's values. A woman can be the harshest judge of another woman's looks, as much as any man. To what extent you let your looks rule your life is a personal decision, but for women, it's still a bigger deal.

I'm aware that by writing a screenwriting book for an industry in which actresses are routinely beautiful, and for the most part need to stay young looking in order to keep working, I'm touching on a paradoxical situation. Thankfully more and more stories are being written for women characters in which their conventional beauty isn't top priority. What about Nanny McPhee? Now it would be truly amazing if a man fell in love with her!

How can Adornment function as a phase in the story?

Self-Consciousness

The first and most obvious way is by having your heroine agonize over her self-image. This is the classic externalization of the desire to please along with a whole bunch of anxieties about projecting the wrong image. Your female audience will easily relate to this. It is also refreshing to have heroines who are remarkable by their confidence and love of their physical body, without being conventionally beautiful.

Turning It Around

You can also work out the things your heroine might find beautiful in a man. Objectification of men by heroines is still in its early days on screen, particularly in movies. Jane Campion and Nancy Meyers both are skilled in capturing individual male beauty from the point of view their heroines. In *The Holiday*, manipulative Jasper does have a boyish charm that renders Iris defenseless. As for Jude Law's widower? He's meltingly open and vulnerable, and that's his facial features alone.

Beauty Is in the Eye of the Culture

Every culture has different attitudes about beauty. Think about what your story says about female beauty from a cultural point of view. Maybe you think it's one of the most desirable assets for all women, and there's nothing wrong with that.

Ugly Ducklings

In *The Devil Wears Prada*, heroine Andrea dips her toe in the sea of superficiality and *doesn't* permanently transform. She reverts to her unfashionable image by the end of the film and reclaims that part of herself. But she still looks good; this is Ann Hathaway after all. It's great when actresses can go all the way and genuinely transform, and you can write this into your script. Pull no punches about the reality of your heroine's looks. Virginia Woolf had a big nose and messy hair. Frida Kahlo had a moustache and monobrow. Both women had their own forms of beauty that grew from their beautiful minds and refusal to accept conventional standards.

Bigger Women

Thankfully there's been a rise in actresses who are naturally larger on our screens. Charlize Theron's transformation in *Monster*, in which she piled on the pounds, made her female character all the more plausible.

Precious is a groundbreaking film that I refer to a great deal. On the beauty front it leaves me in two minds. I understand that obesity in Precious reflects her self-hate and her mother's force feeding, and maybe she is just one of these naturally larger women who are alienated because of their weight. I like the fact that as her self-esteem grows her outer self manifests her inner self. She looks happier and is out of the sweat pants and hoodies despite her total poverty. However, you can't help but feel there's a shock tactic going on, that her weight and size are on one level gratuitous for the audience, that there could be a correlation between her victim-status and her obesity. The first time I watched *Precious* I was with an audience of largely teenage girls (it was an educational screening). When Precious' breast came out to feed the baby, the audience of girls screamed in repulsed horror. I thought it was sad that young girls are so image obsessed they couldn't see it as a tender moment.

Older Women

If your heroine is older, the Adornment phase might reflect her feelings of redundancy in the looks department, or you might choose her to be a champion of self-love. If the latter, you can break a great deal of acceptable clichés! Nobody is happy about aging, men or women, but not everybody wants to drink at the Fountain of Eternal Youth either.

Tips for Writing Identity Phases

Introducing Your Heroine

The first time she enters her story, make a point of mentioning her dominant attitude first, and then focus on her unique features. An actress will thank you for distinguishing features, not universally desired ones.

Your Heroine's Self-Esteem as a Woman

Who were your heroine's first female role models? What did they feel about her? How does she feel about being a woman? Did she internalize these values? Write a scene in which your heroine reveals how she feels about herself as a woman by action or attitudes.

Remember the Maternal Lessons and Father Distance are metaphoric principles. You don't have to give your character an actual mother in her story. Does your character feel comfortable around women, or does she prefer the company of men? Write a scene in which she is only with other women and focus on her conscious and unconscious attitudes toward these women. Remember the Maternal Lessons can be helpful and unhelpful to your heroine. Like Maternal Lessons, your heroine's father doesn't actually have to feature in your story.

What are her values about women's status in society? If your heroine was asked how she would describe sexism in her culture, what would she say? Is she a feminist, seeing misogyny and sexual double standards everywhere she looks? Is she ultrafeminine? Or does she consider herself as being just normal? How does her life mirror her mother's, and how has she made changes? Write a scene in which she confronts her mother's attitudes.

An Identity Phase in Close-Up

The Secret Life of Bees

Lily creeps away from her abusive father's house at night and runs to a private place in the garden. There, she secretly digs up some possessions of her dead mother. Lily has a ritual of putting on a pair of her mother's gloves, taking out a photograph of her mother, and lying down on the ground. She then places the photograph on her bare stomach and holds it, as a pregnant woman holds her own baby inside her. Lily talks to her mother the whole time, almost conversationally, reminiscing about the way her mother used to care for her.

In this scene, Lily's Maternal Lessons that she tells herself are that her mother loved her, cared for her, and never wanted to be apart from her. A woman is a safe haven, someone who would never abandon or hurt her. Lily carries this lesson closely to her heart and on her journey. It makes the unbearable bearable, even the fact that Lily accidentally shot her mother dead when she was a baby. It shows Lily's basic orientation toward women as one of trust and affinity. She literally craves the warmth of women described in her Maternal Lessons.

THE RELATING PHASES

The Relating phases relate to your heroine's actions, attitudes, needs, and emotions about her relationships. They show how other people influence her sense of identity and the reasons behind her relationship choices. The Relating Phases are Self-Relegation, Desire for Union, Loving Too Much, and Retreat:

- ∞ The Self-Relegation phase reflects your heroine putting other people's needs second to her own.

- ∞ The Desire for Union phase reflects your heroine's need for intimacy and emotional support, whether platonic, romantic, or sexual.

- ∞ Loving Too Much is the phase in your story in which your heroine's love of another has an overwhelming impact on her identity and decisions.

∾ Retreat is the phase in your story in which your heroine needs to hunker down into herself and only relate to herself.

Self-Relegation

A major part of feminine identity is the requirement for a woman to put her needs second to those she loves, as well as people she doesn't know so well. Men can do this too in relationships, but it isn't such a cultural expectation. That's why we are fascinated and appalled by tough women who defy this and tread on everyone's feelings, like Margaret in *The Proposal*. Being horrible isn't desirable but neither is putting everyone else first — for men or women. With loved ones, the need to Self-Relegate usually is because women are conditioned to be nurturers, a lesson that can be passed on from mother to daughter. Young women in many cultures might feel strong and empowered. Feminism made a great deal of progress for girls who aren't even aware of how things could be different. Sometimes it's not until women become mothers and age that they begin to question the double standard.

Try to work out how your heroine experiences this expectation of women to Self-Relegate. In an ideal world, a girl needs parents who are attune to this expectation of women and will help her build up a strong sense of identity. But in many parts of the world, the wider culture can remind women of their second-class status as citizens.

This need to Self-Relegate one's own needs to be better able to look after other people can pose major internal conflicts for many women, who can feel split between wanting to do things for themselves (while fearing to be seen as selfish) and wanting to be reliable.

Self-Relegation can be quite paralyzing for a girl or woman. It reflects loss of self-esteem for a whole range of reasons. Women who have been married for many years can sometimes develop a huge dependency on their husband for certain tasks, like driving or handling money. This can be disempowering for a woman, and she might not even recognize it until the marriage ends or her husband dies. Then the world can seem like a frightening place for your heroine. A young girl might self-relegate because she is being emotionally or physically abused.

Being at the center of family life because she is the nurturer can lead a woman to overcontrol. When the children don't need her any more it can be a major loss to a woman's identity. The empty-nest syndrome is a painful process in which your heroine might literally feel like part of her has died. This is because the conditioning to look after others is so strong that when your heroine is finally confronted with herself, she finds that there isn't much there.

So how does Self-Regulation work as a phase in your story? Essentially, it's those moments in which your heroine is confronted with the choice to assert her own desires or to do the right thing for others by meeting their needs first.

Fear of Being Judged

Heroines who seek approval from other characters might fear being judged. This stems from a tendency in women to blame themselves for things going wrong, itself a by-product of being the Nurturer. Your heroine might feel that her own behavior has brought a bad situation on herself; if she hadn't done this or done more of that, then this wouldn't have happened. Taking too much responsibility for a situation shows a Relegated Self. This is a classic symptom of self-relegation, when your heroine hasn't been taught good enough Maternal Lessons to make her understand that she doesn't have to blame herself. In *The Accused*, Sarah likes to have a flirt with the guys. But this doesn't mean she is asking to be gang raped. It takes strong-woman Kathryn to persuade Sarah to fight her case.

Protecting the Male Ego

Your heroine might face the dilemma of her needs being a major problem for her male partner. *A Star is Born* is about a rising star whose rise to success threatens the ego of her husband. Their marriage suffers as she tries to balance meeting her needs, as well as keeping him happy. That film might be decades old, but some of the issues are familiar for women who are more successful than their husbands. In *Erin Brockovich*, Erin is eventually left by her boyfriend because she doesn't self-relegate. After one too many sessions looking after her kids, he realizes he's a man, a biker even, who doesn't have to self-relegate any longer for someone so ungrateful and stressed out.

Collusion of the Family

Everyone benefits from the heroine, in the role choice of Nurturer, self-relegating. It is human nature not to resist something that makes our lives easier. Some women really do need their partners and children to encourage them to do more for themselves, otherwise they would never give themselves permission. If Self-Relegation is seriously undermining your heroine, it can often be linked to the Eruption phase (see following text). She might walk out like Shirley Valentine (in *Shirley Valentine*) or snap aggressively, the way Carrie does in the TV episode of *Sex and the City*, when Aidan first moves into her flat, and it dawns on her that she can't write with his constant need to interact. The Self-Relegating part of her at first tries to be nice, but then she erupts. Assertion of what you need has to take place, but often Eruption in the form of maternal meltdown is a very common way women point out to their families that they've had enough.

Unconscious Self-Sabotage

Your heroine may make odd choices seen in the light of what might be good for her own ego, but in another light they might be good for her relationship, even her own survival. Passivity is frustrating in a heroine, but it might be a logical reaction to an oppressive situation. Self-sabotage is about blowing your own chances out of fear of what it might do to your relationship. This is frequently seen in heroines who have fear-of-abandonment issues. Paradoxically, the heroine's partner might actually want the heroine to go out and achieve something. If he's sensitive, he might have to go out of his way to prove it to her. Or your heroine may have chosen a man who believes looking after the home is a shared task.

A Strong Ego

You might want your heroine to have high self-esteem and be extra-alert to any issues that might make her put up and shut up. She doesn't care what people might call her, she's going to do things her way. *Erin Brockovich* is interesting in this respect, because on one hand we all know why she's a fighter, and we know why she's got to get out of her situation. On the other hand, it is still hard to watch her blow her relationship when she won't back down. Erin's own inner battle with maternal guilt shows her conflict regarding Self-Relegation. Has she gone so far that she's hurting her children? It's a tough call for the strong woman.

Don't forget many women don't see Self-Relegation as negative. They see it as their natural role as wives and mothers.

Desire for Union

This phase is all about your heroine's desire for love or intimacy, whether it's for a lifetime or one night. As I'm sure you're aware, it is one of the strongest phases in the vast majority of heroines' stories, in which relationships are central. This is because of the Nurturing role choice that women are conditioned to follow from a very young age, the Maternal Lessons and Father Distance issues that orient women to needing love and affirmation of love, and all the cultural messages that bombard women's lives. In this respect, it can last a whole story, or be momentary, depending on who your heroine is, what she wants, and how a "union" fits into her life during the story. A heroine's self-esteem is dependent on the amount of close and supportive relationships, in the form of friends, loving family members, lovers, and long-term partners.

As a shorter phase, it can take the form of a bad date, one-night stand, chat with a friendly stranger in the ladies rest room, girl's night out, and glance across a crowded room. The desire for the touch of another, even if your heroine has just met him or her, can reveal a great deal about her state of mind and her character.

Being Ready

Sometimes, when a heroine has spent enough time in retreat, she is ready to form a new relationship or at least explore the possibility. In *Under the Tuscan Sun*, Desire for Union only becomes possible for the heroine in the last sequence of the story, which is all about getting over a traumatic breakup. Your heroine can stumble into the phase, for example by meeting someone unexpectedly, and before you know it, she's longing for a relationship.

Ambivalence

In *The Upside of Anger*, the heroine experiences various levels of Desire for Union. She has casual sex with her lover, who she never really emotionally lets in because she is preoccupied with her bitterness over her husband's desertion. By the end, she achieves a much stronger and deeper Desire for Union with her lover, finally appreciating and needing him. Casual sex is a major theme of *Under the Skin*, in which the heroine deals with the loss of her mother by needing physical sex as an annihilation of her emotional pain.

We Are Family

Family scenes, which show the sense of belonging a heroine feels, are very common in this phase. The heroine may feel happy to be with her family, and conflict can be generated by her sensing that her partner feels uncomfortable. She wants him to belong too! Loving friends can also symbolize a family group that the heroine needs for validation and support.

Marriage

A wedding is a symbolic fulfilment of the Desire for Union, but a marriage is the ultimate test of the durability of that desire. The many tests of love during a marriage — children, stress, either partners or one partner changing, changes in the wider world, or poverty — can seriously make each partner question where the love has gone. In *The Painted Veil*, Kitty marries to get away from her family, knowing she is not in love with her husband. Soon she experiences the phase of the Desire for Union by having a passionate affair with a married man. When she finds out that her lover is not going to leave his wife for her, she has no choice but to follow her deeply hurt husband to a town infected with cholera. Over the next few months, she sees a new side to her husband, and the seeds of Desire for Union with him finally grow in the most testing of circumstances. The reversal of her feelings is symbolized by a need for sex, but it is clear that she has now fallen in love with him because she has matured sufficiently to see his strengths.

Lost Union

The Desire for Union phase is at its most moving when the heroine's loved one has died, and the yearning cannot be satisfied except by memory. In *P.S. I Love You*, the heroine's mourning is made all the more poignant and yearning because of the letters her husband wrote before he died, to help her get over the loss.

Loving Too Much

This phase is akin to Self-Relegation in that the heroine experiences a loss of identity and a grip on herself. The difference is that Loving Too Much is a result of either obsessional love, overprotective love, or an unhealthy desire for love. Whatever the cause, it reveals an internal imbalance in the heroine.

Obsessional Love

This can take many forms in a story, from heartbreak, getting over someone, needing a boyfriend to fill some kind of internal vacuum or emptiness, to a monumental crush. It's when the heroine loses perspective because of love and consequently loses a grip on herself.

Denigratory Love

Love can be bad for your heroine when the relationship has gone wrong and destroys her self-esteem. "Love" can still exist in a form of familiarity and need for security. It's the syndrome of "better the devil you know." The mother in *East Is East* loves her husband, but he is violent toward her and tyrannical. The Loving Too Much phase forms the basis of a great deal of her scenes, in which she wrestles with her internal conflict over her husband's unacceptable behavior. Should she leave him? Can she stand up to him? Similarly, the heroine in *Shirley Valentine* puts up with being underappreciated for too long for the sake of Loving Too Much before she walks out of her life.

Risk Taking

The Loving Too Much phase can make a heroine take enormous risks. In *Elizabeth,* risk-taking Queen Elizabeth sleeps with her lover, thus debunking the myth that she was England's Virgin Queen. Her ladies-in-waiting know, and the court gossips. Her advisors know she cannot marry him, so she must not risk pregnancy.

Parental Love

Can we love our children too much? When it stifles their development and becomes more about fulfilling our needs and anxieties, as opposed to theirs. Overprotective parents tend to have unresolved wounds from their own childhood. They could have been emotionally or physically neglected. Or they are simply control freaks, who sow the seeds of their own misfortune because their child will escape as soon as she has enough independence. The mother who is jealous of the second wife or the stepmom of her children Loves Too Much in an unhealthy way. You can use this phase in scenes and sequences in which this problem generates lots of conflict between parents and children.

Retreat

The need to retreat could be a reaction to grief, trauma, or despair, or it could be a time to have fun or a quiet time with herself. Maybe she's a mother and feels like she's at everyone's beck and call, or she's sick and tired of juggling. Maybe she just wants to feel like herself, without all the pressures or roles she has to play in life. Physical reasons can include biological changes that all women go through. Or they could be due to sickness or other problems. Your heroine will need to withdraw from the world, her friends, even her lover, because for whatever reason she needs to be alone. Retreat helps her replenish herself. Retreat can be a lifestyle choice if she has no trust or affection for others.

Loss

The acute pain of losing a loved one is the hardest thing for your heroine to bear. If it's her child, lover, another close family member, or best friend, she will feel it like a mortal wound. The bereavement process requires withdrawal, except when the heroine is actively in denial of her pain.

After Trauma

Retreat is a phase that can be a scene or two long, last a sequence, or literally drive a huge part of the story. In *I've Loved You So Long*, Juliette takes a whole film to come out of a self-imposed psychological and physical retreat from life. So great is her emotional pain, she does nothing to resist going to prison for fifteen years.

Enforced Retreat

Any form of incarceration against your heroine's will is an enforced retreat. The twist can be when a heroine is imprisoned by the authorities because of a *crime passionel*, as in the case of the French heroines of *I've Loved You So Long* and *Leaving*. Both women commit crimes for love. This phase can happen in the backstory or future. The ambivalent nature of how a heroine relates to Enforced Retreat can be seen in stories with rehab clinics, where she doesn't really want to be, but some part of her knows it is for her own good, as in *28 Days* and *Rachel Getting Married*.

Biological Changes

Women's reproductive processes and biology can often bring about a need to Retreat, even if it's momentary. From menstruation to breastfeeding, women have lots of regular reminders of their bodies' needs and cycles. Your heroine can view them as a nuisance, try to ignore them (*Boys Don't Cry*), be ashamed of them, or celebrate and love her physical processes as part of her essential, female being.

Finding the Self

Sometimes a heroine needs to be alone if her external life expects her to be too many things to too many people. This is the case with Elizabeth II in *The Queen*. The Retreat phase is extended in the story because Elizabeth needs to be human, not regal. Alone in the Scottish Highlands, the Retreat phase leads her to self-discovery and self-truth. Fame is another extremely testing challenge for some heroines. They may need Retreat to keep in touch with who they truly are. Trying to be something for others, putting on a different mask to hide who she really is, can lead to a character needing to Retreat in order to be themselves.

Secret Rites

People can retreat to be themselves and do things in private that are unacceptable to others or that they are ashamed of, all of which help them survive life. Self-mutilation is a very private act, as is binge eating and bulimia.

Tips for Writing Relating Phases

Emotions

Get inside your character's head in the scene to really know what she is feeling about the other person. Try to make it specific to exactly that moment in time. Emotions can be paradoxical and ambivalent. Your heroine might be really angry and want sex at the same time. She might be evaluating the risk of union the whole time she's actively seeking it.

Actions Speak Louder Than Words

In an intense Relating scene or sequence, write the whole scene in dialogue. If your heroine is on her own, write out what she's thinking as a monologue. Highlight all the strongest emotions in the speech. Then rewrite the whole scene, with no dialogue or monologue, just action. If you focus on the highlighted speech and turn that into action, you will be amazed how many nonverbal ways you can find to convey the emotion.

Settings

Relating phases work well in settings that intensify the emotions. The setting can do this by providing extreme contrast, or by mirroring the emotions and identity issues that face your heroine. Let's take female bonding, for example. It's very common to see female bonding scenes in spas or at the nail, beauty, or hair salon. This underlines the sense of conventional femininity. Alternatively, you could contrast a female bonding scene by putting two women executives in a boardroom full of men, where they show empathy to one another through a minor gesture. These principles don't just apply to female bonding. They apply to all aspects of Relating.

Power Dynamics

Contrary to much screenwriting opinion, I believe there is a place in a story for a moment to exist for what it is, as opposed to a transaction happening. A scene doesn't necessarily need a shift in values or power. Scenes do not have to have a turning point or reflect a metaphoric "deal" taking place between characters. A moment of love or happiness is just that. We are trained to think of these as expositional empty beats when really they can be holistic and transcendental moments that are important and pleasurable to the audience. They are moments of peace, acceptance, quietness, and love.

A Relating Phase in Close-Up

Julie and Julia

In *Julie and Julia*, there is a sequence I call the Dorothy sequence. *Julie and Julia* is a Feel Good Femininity Film, full of joy and harmony; accordingly, the phases that are most visible throughout the film are those that dwell on the positive. This sequence shows how the phases can be used to help you at the very detailed level of a scene. (For explanation of phases I haven't covered yet, but refer to here, read on!)

Dorothy is Julia's sister and has been invited by Julia to stay with her and her husband Paul in Paris where they live. The sequence starts as Julia and Paul wait at the train station for Dorothy. This is the Path to Potential phase. Will Dorothy come, and how will the visit go? The other phase is Desire for Union. Julia loves and misses her sister, and is keen to see her. As Dorothy appears, even taller than Julia, the women are delighted to see each other, full of joy, their Desire for Union fulfilled! Desire for Union continues over lunch, but is interwoven with the Father Distance phase as they discuss their relationships with their father, who disapproves of their life choices. "He wanted us to move to Pasadena, marry republicans and breed like rabbits." Instead both women are childless and radical. The Path to Potential phase underpins the party Julia holds for Dorothy, to "match make" her with a man even taller than her. Dorothy shows she has a Desire for Union with a very short man instead, providing a moment of humor. Desire for Union continues at the wedding between Dorothy and her man, in which Julia is the bridesmaid. At the reception, Julia is confronted with her Father Distance as she sits with her father at the meal. He is busy criticizing Dorothy's choice of husband. Avoiding an Eruption, Julia gets up to dance, which is a Retreat from her father. Sometime after the wedding, a letter comes from Dorothy. She's pregnant. Julia cries, retreating into Paul's arms for nurturing because she can't have babies. This is a tough Maternal Lesson she has learned. Instead of babies, Julia will commit to the Path to Potential by writing her book.

THE MOMENTUM PHASES

The Momentum phase in your heroine's story is the time when she has to take action in order to move forward. They focus on your heroine's need to make progress and transform her life. These phases can frequently be associated with dramatic action, such as inciting incidents, turning points, and climaxes. The Momentum Phases are Violation, Crossroads, Eruption, and Path to Potential:

∞ The Violation phase reflects your heroine's experience of being aggressed or being the aggressor.

∞ The Crossroads phase reflects the time when your heroine is presented with several choices, each of which will take her life in a completely different direction.

∞ The Eruption phase reflects your heroine's need to explode as a reaction to repression.

∞ The Path to Potential phase symbolizes your heroine making a choice of direction for her life.

Violation

At some early point in a woman's life she comes to terms with the fact that she might not be able to defend herself from assault, violence, rape, or abuse. Men might fear attack, but women fear sexual attack. The ratio of men being attacked by dildo-wielding rapist women compared to men raping women is exceedingly rare. I have seen a comic spoof of this in *Weeds*. A dramatic version of female rape is in *Girl with the Dragon Tattoo*, but this is a retaliatory rape. What women actually do to violate men sexually is to castrate, and that's still an exceedingly rare crime compared to rape. It tends to be a retaliatory impulse when a woman has had enough of philandering.

The trouble with a fear of violation is that it teaches women to fear their own sexual power and desire. Women then associate sexuality with vulnerability. Maybe it is this sense of vulnerability in women that makes them all the more sensitive to betrayal. "Hell hath no fury" is probably one of Shakespeare's most overused quotations. I'm not suggesting men don't feel betrayal acutely, but maybe they feel it differently. If a man is sexually betrayed by his partner he might have some condolence in remembering that women's philandering has been punishable by men for several thousand years. Today he can brand his partner a slut and still have a better chance of keeping his kids in the divorce courts. In the Middle East a woman can still be stoned to death. A woman who is raped can sometimes be accused of bringing it on herself. Double standards sadly persist.

The message we all grow up with is that women not only have to control their own sexual behavior, but also they're responsible for a man's libidinous self-control. Violation as a phase symbolizes this threat, whether it's real or actual. Betrayal is one of its most obvious forms. A man cheats or lets the heroine down in some way. Whatever the cause, she feels wounded to the core of her being. There are heroines who have such pride that they don't admit to being wounded, but these are rare. If she is in denial, it usually becomes part of her journey to finally admit these feelings.

Violation can also take the form of abuse by parent figures, whether it's emotional or physical. In *Precious*, Precious experiences years of abuse from both her parents. However, she is not completely passive in life, defending her white and male teacher by beating up a male student in class.

But there's a flipside to the coin — where the Violation phase is perpetuated by the woman. Women can and do beat up their husbands. Women commit infanticide or self-mutilate. Killing one's children, the Medea complex, can be motivated by an extremely irrational need to punish the children's father. Teen girls can join violent gangs. Female anger and rage, and their violation of other people, is not as acceptable in stories as women being on the receiving end. With Precious having a violent fight with her mother, and the two heroines of *Frozen River* at each other's throats, I believe that a shift in the lack of representation of women's anger and violence is finally taking place in movies. On TV, the officers in *CSI: Crime Scene Investigation* are used to the murderous impulses of many a female violator. Tarantino's heroines are very violent, as are the girls of *St. Trinian's*, but these are unrealistic and glorified.

Crossroads

Every time we make a choice, evaluating our different options, we are at a kind of Crossroads in our lives. *If I do this, this might happen. But if I do that instead, they maybe I will or won't get this.* Crossroads are ego-driven dilemmas that reflect heroines' decision-making processes. They are very subjective, and tend to reveal your heroine's value system and her sense of identity. Decisions made by characters under pressure are a staple of drama, but Crossroads can be very different for women, and so for your female character. Major life choices include how and when to have children (knowing that it isn't a lifetime option); whether to have an abortion or not; what man to marry; staying single; what profession; staying at home with the kids or putting career first; giving up your whole life for the person you love. Minor choices can be as simple as: Should I drive or walk? If I eat that cake, will I regret it later? The black dress or the red?

As a story progresses, the Crossroads phases, of which there will be many, reflect the growth in your heroine. As she gets to know herself better, what would have once been a difficult dilemma is now no longer relevant to her. This is true to life. As we age and get to know ourselves, we tend to make better choices that suit our true identity. But we can also get risk averse, or frightened of change. A heroine who makes choices to challenge herself shows an adventurous spirit.

New Directions

Crossroads can lead to Path to Potential and Transitions. By making certain choices the heroine can enter completely new worlds. Maria in *Maria Full of Grace* has the choice of unemployment, caring for a family that takes her for granted, another exploitative job in her community, or becoming a drug mule. Once she becomes a drug mule, she is eventually led to a Path to Potential of a new life on her own in the U.S.

Devastating Crossroads

In *Sophie's Choice*, Sophie has to make the unbearable decision about which child to let die at the hands of Nazis. Of course, there is no answer to this horrifying dilemma, but under unbearable pressure she impulsively pushes her son toward the soldier. It is an unforgettable and harrowing Crossroads moment in movie history. Sophie will never get over this decision, and it will eventually lead to her suicide.

Eruption

The Eruption phase is a potentially cathartic phase in your story when everything bursts out into the open. It symbolizes the energetic and needed emotional, physical, verbal, or social outburst that leads to change. Usually a tipping point has been reached by your heroine before this phase occurs. Eruption is a two-fold phase. First, the lid is blown off, and then the contents settle. The settling can be as short or as long as your story needs.

Trying to please everyone all of the time can cause major pressure in a woman's life. Multitasking has its downsides. This isn't about women not being able to take pressure, it can be about women not being able to say no or in no position to say no so they can single-mindedly focus on one thing.

Your heroine might endure an Eruption as a result of her own repression. What she thought was an adequate coping mechanism is faulty after all, and it cracks under the pressure. Eruption can be fueled by a growing sense of identity crisis. It can seem as if every path is blocked, and all your heroine can do is metaphorically scream out loud. Alternatively she can fight, walk away, or break down. Breakdowns usually lead to breakthroughs, in our own behavior and in the behavior of others around us.

However, Eruption is only as healing as your heroine or other characters want to make it. Some wounds are opened, only to heal over, thus keeping the poison inside. Sometimes a huge mess is left, but your heroine might move on and let others pick up the pieces. It's a bit like throwing your cards on the table. The truth is out for all to see, and there's no going back to the same game.

Frequently the most powerful eruption in a story corresponds to the climax in act 3 of a linear screenplay. However, there can be many climaxes in many heroines' stories, particularly complex-linear screenplays.

Eruption as a Cry for Help

In *Rachel Getting Married*, the heroine Kym cannot take her self-hate anymore. Her Eruption takes the form of a fight with her mother (blowing the lid) and then driving her car into a tree (the dust settling). Although she could have killed herself, her real need is to make people understand the depth of her misery for being responsible for her little brother's death.

Maternal Meltdown

The opposite situation from a cry for help is when a heroine erupts as a need to escape, literally or metaphorically. She feels she has nothing to lose. In *East Is East*, the mother and wife of the family finally snaps and stands up to her bully of a husband. She is at a point where it is impossible to keep living by his rules.

Momentary Madness

This is where the Eruption phase appears instantly and shoots out of nowhere. Your heroine might suffer a momentary lack of impulse control, which can set a spiral of events in motion. She might shoot someone and surprise herself in the process. When Thelma and Louise look at each other as their car approaches the cliff top, they share a final and impulsive moment of Eruption.

A Very Long Eruption

Because of their two-stage nature, Eruptions can be very drawn out. The dust settling might take over her story. In *Villa Amalia*, Ann drives to a car park and screams a primal scream after realizing her partner has been having an affair. The majority of the film is all concerned with the dust settling as she detaches, slowly but surely, from every part of her life in one long Eruption.

Eruption and Violation

A fight between two characters can seem like a Violation phase but normally the Violation is the tipping point that leads to a heroine erupting. In *Precious*, Precious returns from the hospital with her newborn baby only to realize the danger her mother presents if Precious continues to let her mother victimize her. Precious's tipping point is realizing that her mother will take her son from her and ruin the first good thing in her life that she has done for herself. This is Precious' Eruption, and it leads to her mother's violent assault. The dust settling takes the form of Precious fighting back and finally fleeing.

Path to Potential

Path to Potential can be like the connective tissue of your heroines' journey, linking the phases of Identity and Relating to each other. They are the times when she takes steps and strives for something with a sense of purposefulness with the belief that she is doing the right thing, at that given moment. It's about positive energy and direction in the story.

The whole point is that the character feels in control, unlike Transition, which has more unconsciously propelling forces behind it and involves loss of identity. By taking the Path to Potential, your heroine feels like she is making this happen. Your heroine has a game plan, and she's pursuing it.

Your heroine might choose the wrong Path to Potential and end up facing labyrinths, dead-ends, and crossroads. It's a guaranteed certainty she will, if she is really out of touch with what she needs. In this respect, a Path to Potential will only be as helpful to a heroine as her levels of self-knowledge and insight will allow. For example, in *An Education*, Jenny takes the Path to Potential when she walks out of school thinking her engagement to a rich man will bring her far more than an Oxford education ever will. If she has unresolved issues, the Path to Potential can lead to disaster. Think of women with low self-esteem who go from man to man always in the hope that the next one is Mr. Right, only to be repeating the same relationship mistakes. The only right path for this kind of woman is to spend some time walking alone to get to know herself better.

Final Paths

Many heroines' stories end with the heroine taking a final Path to Potential. She isn't returning anywhere familiar, she is moving on. In *Frozen River*, the heroine Ray ends her journey by going to prison, while Lila finally reclaims her stolen child and moves into Ray's brand new mobile home to take care of her friend's kids while she's in prison. Many heroines keep moving on at the end of the story. They have found a new sense of identity but have yet to find a place they can belong. Sometimes a heroine has unfinished business with herself. She's got to keep moving to find a place where she can belong. Katherine Ann in *Mona Lisa Smile* is this kind of heroine, a true nomad who likes a life full of Paths to Potential.

Many heroines never go home at the end of their story. Your heroine might still not have found the place where she belongs, or she is still unsure about what she really wants from life. She might have resolution on some levels, but not all, and she has to keep moving. Pippa Lee in *The Secret Lives of Pippa Lee* is one heroine who knows only what she doesn't want to be anymore.

Tips for Writing Momentum Phases

Image Systems

In your scenes, generate imagery that symbolizes the loss of the old or the birth of the new. Or even both. For example, if your character is on her way to a new job that will require her to abandon all her values, you can foreshadow the imminent culture clash even before your heroine has arrived. The opening sequence of *The Devil Wears Prada* is a good example of using imagery that suggests change is afoot as we see a montage of morning rituals of very different women getting ready for work. You want to choose images that deepen your scene symbolically. This will help your audience get a sense of your character's state of mind during the change.

Emotional Changes

Change is not a static process. Your heroine will experience fluctuating changes through scenes with Momentum phases. What is she feeling, remembering, regretting, or excited about? Write them!

Clothes

What is your heroine wearing? Clothes can really say a great deal about the inner emotional state of your heroine. What statement are your heroine's clothes making about the momentum? This isn't about stealing the costume designer's thunder; it's about making sure that the scene is rich with meaning on a psychological level.

Possessions

What does your heroine take with her? What objects does she bring that make her feel secure in herself? Do these possessions represent a new self or are they comforting baggage from the past? Are any of these possessions instrumental in the change? Does she need them to pull it off?

The Momentum Phase in Close-Up

The Hours

Laura (Julianne Moore) has decided to take her own life, so unbearable is her existence to her. On the way to the babysitter, Laura pulls away, driving past a removal lorry, as another family is moving into the suburban neighborhood. Laura's son knows something is wrong, perceptive to his mother's mood. He screams as she walks away from the childminder's house, and Laura is distressed. She drives manically, and suddenly swerves dangerously, pulling into a hotel complex. Meanwhile, the son is building a house with his toys, only to destroy it. A sense of calm and purpose spreads over Laura's face as she approaches the hotel. She asks for a room where she won't be disturbed. Once alone, she lies on the bed and gets various bottles of pills and a book, *Mrs. Dalloway* by Virginia Woolf, out of her purse. As Laura touches her bare pregnant stomach, pond water full of leaves suddenly surges into the room, covering Laura, a visually metaphoric surge.

This sequence mainly reflects the Eruption phase as Laura decides to take her own life. She can't take her life anymore, but she isn't the kind of character who screams, shouts, and throws things. The image systems (new neighbors moving in, the child's broken toys) clearly show the destruction of the home, which foreshadow what will happen to Laura's own family once she dies. As she drives she is taking a Path to Potential — escape by death. The possessions (tablets, the novel) are essential in order to bring about the desired change, death. Her loosening of her clothes and baring herself deepens the sense of change. In terms of role choices, Laura starts the sequence as a Mother and a Victim, and soon is a Questing Heroine with a very clear sense of purpose as she approaches the hotel. Later, the experience of Eruption forces her to adjust back to accepting her Maternal Lessons, by sticking to the role choice of Mother as she decides she cannot take her own life. We find out by the end of the film that Eruption made her modify her quest; instead of taking her life, she abandoned her children. This Eruption phase ends up with Laura clearing out some poison of her psychological wound, but it is still festering.

EXERCISE: PHASES IN A COMPLEX-LINEAR FILM

Looking at the phases in a nonlinear film will help you see that they can really help you develop your heroine's emerging identity in the story, at the same time as you develop your theme. Complex linear stories are all about theme. By showing different timescales, they invite you to think about themes that affect women's lives more than be gripped to watching the pursuit of a goal, as many linear films show. *La Vie en Rose* is a great example of a complex linear film. It has three interweaving storylines: one with the child Edith, one with an adult Edith striving for and achieving success, and one with Edith nearing the end of her life.

Your exercise now is to watch *La Vie en Rose* and see if you can identify which phases are going on in each of the three story lines. Get ready to press the pause, and have a pen and lots of paper on hand. While you are doing this, try to work out which role choices Edith the heroine relates to.

Then work out which phases might shape your heroine's sense of identity during the course of her story. Which appeal to you most, and why? Which are useful to develop your backstory?

WOMEN IN TROUBLE

Chapter 6

Conflict is basically a clash between two opposed viewpoints. That clash can be physical, mental, verbal, emotional, relational, territorial, ideological, political, national and international, and even intergalactic. Conflict can be healthy, destructive, annihilating, preventable, unnecessary, or necessary.

Whatever it is, conflict is part of life. How you manage conflict in your own life will depend on your personality, belief systems, and self-control. Even if you choose a peaceful path in life, conflict can follow you. Your relationship might suddenly end; you might lose a loved one, your job, money, or health; you might be attacked physically, sexually, or verbally; your country might go to war. All these can and do present obstacles in our lives; it is part of being human. An attitude of acceptance, tolerance, and forgiveness might help you get through the conflict, but the conflict still has to be borne in some way.

When it comes to storytelling, we're often told that conflict is the primary building block of all dramatic stories, whatever their genre. No conflict makes a story boring. *What's at stake? What's the threat? What does she have to lose? Who's the bad guy?* These are familiar and often very important questions in the writing process. If you're writing a heroine's story, conflict can be treated very differently, for the simple reason women's lives are very different from men's. It's up to you as the writer to work out how that difference is played out in your story. So when it comes to conflict, I'm not taking on the perceived wisdom of Western dramatic theory — which works very well for certain kinds of stories, genres, and audiences — but I do want to give you a different way of thinking about conflict for your heroine's story.

CULTURAL CONFLICT

The first thing to be aware of is how your own cultural attitudes and expectations will have an impact on your writing. Your own cultural values will affect

∾ Your heroine's culture.

∾ Your own cultural background.

∾ The culture of the audience you want to reach.

Let's take a closer look at two very different heroines' stories to illustrate this point. The first film is *At Five in the Afternoon*. The story is set in post-9/11 Afghanistan and follows the dreams of Nogreh, who decides she wants to be president of Afghanistan. Every kind of obstacle is against her dream. Her father is a religious fundamentalist who is against education of women. The family has no money. The community has very rigid and repressive codes for female behavior. Nogreh secretly wears white high-heeled shoes under her burqa as an act of defiance and to make her feel feminine in a way that isn't allowed in her culture. When she slips the shoes on, even though they are ingrained with mud and battered, you sense she feels empowered by one small step away from her oppressive existence. To some audiences, her old shoes could seem like pathetic symbols of a life Nogreh will never be able to have; to others, they might represent hope. Although Nogreh starts out with a dream, it's her gradual sense of disillusion that breaks her. She finally accepts that her aspirations are futile in the male-dominated and fundamentalist system she lives under.

The second is *Confessions of a Shopaholic*. The heroine Rebecca has an uncontrollable addiction to fashion and brand labels in Manhattan. The film is targeted at young female audiences in a Western culture that is highly materialistic, and where a woman's identity is related to what she owns, wears, and looks like. Rebecca's dream is indulging her need for irresistible clothing. Her obstacles are more internal. She has an addiction to compulsive spending, which is only encouraged by the outside world.

As you can see, conflict and obstacles are very different. For Nogreh, the most powerful forms of conflict are external for most of the story, until she gives up. Her own defeatism becomes an internal form of conflict. But the audience might think she's seen the light and got real.

For Rebecca, her debt and her compulsive spending are problems she must battle, along with the constant threat of the debt collector. But Rebecca chooses to be in denial about the mess she's in. Her internal conflict, her blind spot, generates most of the external problems in her world. She has to keep lying to everyone else, because she's lying to herself. Rebecca has freedom of choice to stop, whereas Nogreh has no power. Nogreh's main source of conflict is external. It leads to her having internal conflict about the futility of her hopes and dreams.

As you can see from both examples, conflict is a very powerful element in a heroine's story. Using conflict effectively boils down to you working out how you want your audience to react to your heroine's situation. Ask yourself:

- ∞ Do you want your audience to sympathize with your heroine's plight?

- ∞ Do you want your audience to question your heroine's motives and hope that she sees the light?

- ∞ Do you want her to transform the world she lives in, so she can be free in any area of her life?

- ∞ Do you want your audience to question the values of the world we live in?

How you develop conflict in your story will have an impact on the message of your story. By getting to know the layers of conflict, and learning how they can function, you can make sure conflict works to support your story intentions.

THE LAYERS OF CONFLICT

The layers of conflict is a model that can help you work out the obstacles found in all levels of your heroine's life. For example, if you want to write about a girl's emotional and physical battle with bulimia, then it is a good idea to think about in what ways her problem is both affected by and affects her closest relationships, her family, her community, and the wider culture.

By thinking each layer through, you will be able to make the right creative choices for your story. The layers of conflict can help you strengthen your characters, so you really know what each character is up against. They can also help you intensify your story's theme and metaphoric wound. The layers of conflict are:

⌒ Layer 1: Internal Conflict

⌒ Layer 2: Significant Other Conflict

⌒ Layer 3: Family Conflict

⌒ Layer 4: Community Conflict

⌒ Layer 5: Culture Conflict

⌒ Layer 6: Nation Conflict

⌒ Layer 7: World Conflict

Layer 1: Internal Conflict

This layer reflects the most private, deepest internal conflict your heroine feels. It represents her most private self. It is the scar tissue that she tries to hide from the world. Heroines who are emotionally wounded, trapped in a situation or a culture that damages their sense of identity, have a battle between expectations and how they really want to live their lives, or have deep ambivalence about choices they are faced with, are all experiencing internal conflict.

Internal conflict is the hardest conflict to write because it is the thoughts and feelings going on inside your heroine's mind. You have to think about the external ways a heroine might reveal her internal conflict. If you don't, you will end up relying on the brilliance of the actress playing her. Lee's self-mutilation in *Secretary* is a good example of a heroine dealing with very complex internal conflicts. Lee is getting a sense of release by cutting herself.

INTERNAL

SIGNIFICANT
OTHER

FAMILY

COMMUNITY

CULTURE

NATION

WORLD

Stories that emphasize internal conflict above all other layers can be very powerful viewing experiences. A great deal of contemporary French films are all about the heroine's internal state of mind and follow the heroine as she inwardly processes her life and relationships. *I've Loved You So Long*, *Leaving*, *Villa Amalia*, *Romance*, and *A Ma Soeur!* are all great examples.

Layer 2: Significant Other Conflict

The second layer relates the conflict generated by your heroine's relationship with her significant other. This does not have to be her lover. It is the person in the story your heroine has the closest relationship with, good or bad. It can be the person she is trying to be close to, with whom she has the most long-standing relationship, or is leaving. It can also be a parent, child, sibling, boss, or colleague — it entirely depends on your story.

The conflict generated by this relationship can take many forms. These include wanting to love or be loved; not realizing they are in love; parent/child dynamics; professional rivalry; betrayal; jealousy; envy; loss; abuse; and victimization. It covers the whole range of emotions that the significant other can trigger in your heroine. *The Painted Veil* is a great example of the many different types of conflict a significant other can create for a heroine. In the course of one story, Kitty uses her husband; despises him; cheats on him; is dependent on him; begins to get to know him; becomes angry with him; ultimately falls deeply in love with him; and loses him to cholera. Sometimes, in the course of your story, your heroine's significant other will change. In *The Devil Wears Prada*, Andrea's significant other starts out as Nate, her boyfriend. But he is soon overtaken in this role by Miranda, her controlling boss.

Layer 3: Family Conflict

The third layer relates to your heroine's family and the problems that family life and relationships can cause. The "family" can mean who your heroine thinks of as her real family. Sometimes we choose who we consider as family, particularly if family life has been hateful or abusive, or if you've lost all your real family. This doesn't mean you can ever entirely forget your real family, but you can get love and support in a family way from other people. As many women's lives revolve around their families in their role as mothers, the family is a very common source of conflict in heroines' stories. If she loves them or hates them, your heroine's family will be a massive factor in who she is.

Family conflict can simply take the form of unresolved issues in your heroine's backstory, and these could be spilling out into the story by her way of handling problems in the here and now. Family life gives your heroine her earliest experiences and role models. She has been formed by these, so it pays to know the good, the bad, and the ugly in your heroine's life. Most of Precious' emotional problems stem from her immediate family members. Orphans, adopted children, and sci-fi-manufactured children will have wildly different experiences of family life.

Layer 4: Community Conflict

The fourth layer relates to the community your heroine belongs to. This can be the actual area or her work environment. It's basically her life in a wider setting, beyond the emotional sphere of her family environment. If your heroine's significant other is someone she works with, then lots of additional conflict can be caused in her professional community. *Freedom Writers* is a great example of a heroine overcoming numerous obstacles in her work with deprived teenagers. Problems can take the form of professional rivalry; failure; loss of status in the community; not fitting in with the community's values and mores; and annihilation of the community through war or illness. Many tragic love stories are caused by the community not being able to tolerate the heroine's love affair.

Layer 5: Culture Conflict

Cultural values can cause big problems for your heroine if she doesn't fit in with these, or she can't stop questioning them. The problems caused by cultural values can create a great deal of internal conflict. For example, for many women who do not fit conventional aspects of beauty, the pressure to be slim, young, and beautiful can take its toll. In *The Truth About Cats & Dogs*, the heroine Abby, a radio presenter, feels too fat and ugly to take her chances with a sexy guy who listens to her show and who has fallen in love with her personality. Inadequacy rules the day, and the presenter persuades her conventionally attractive but highly unintelligent friend to pretend to be her, with disastrous consequences.

Pressure to marry, stay married, and be a good mother can all create massive problems for your heroine if she's in a bad situation. Sexism and racism are also cultural values that might affect her life negatively. Being from a good enough family, having the right education, and knowing social etiquette are at the end of the day privileged circumstances that your heroine might not be lucky enough to have been born with.

Layer 6: Nation Conflict

The conflict created at the national level in a story is usually obvious from the lives of the women characters. What is going on for women in a country at a particular time in history is the main issue here. A country's laws and policies go a long way to shaping our lives as women, from reproduction to equality in the workplace. Some of the problems confronting your heroine might be created by the real conditions of the country in which she lives. It can be a good idea to think about the reality of your women's characters lives. *North Country* and *Erin Brockovich* are good examples of women using the American legal system in order to make changes to improve women's and families' lives in the U.S.

On a lighter level, *The Proposal* shows Margaret in a full-on battle with the U.S. immigration services that want to deport her. Her ruthless decision to force her male secretary to marry her gives Margaret problems on every level. From internalized guilt, hostility with an angry significant other, to acting illegally, Margaret is more than preoccupied.

Layer 7: World Conflict

Stories can take on a wide dimension if a sense of the world can somehow be conveyed. All countries have a specific position in the world order, the most obvious examples of the conflict generated by this position are found in war films. Hannah in *The English Patient* loses her Canadian lover due to armed conflict. Elizabeth I wages war and defends her country in *Elizabeth* and the sequel, *Elizabeth: The Golden Age*. The writers of *Confessions of a Shopaholic* could have given a sense of the world by referring to the sweat shops of developing countries producing many brand name goods. *Frozen River* follows a Mohawk woman and a poor white woman taking huge risks to try to improve their family situations by smuggling immigrants into the U.S.

Let's take a look at two very different heroines' stories to see the layers of conflict at work — the mainstream studio film *Twilight* and the low-budget Peruvian film *The Milk of Sorrow*.

Twilight

Internal Conflict

Bella is one of those rare heroines who knows what she wants — to love Edward Cullen, a gorgeous hunk of a vampire. She doesn't care that he's a vampire, and by the end of the narrative, she wants to become one too so they can be together forever. Her main internal conflict is the fact that, by loving Edward, complications have occurred and Bella's family is now in jeopardy. Neither can she tell her family about her love. It is too shocking, and they would take action to remove her from Forks where she lives.

Significant Other Conflict

This is the primary source of conflict in *Twilight*. There is a forbidden and impossible aspect to their love for each other. Edward's desire for human blood might make him want to kill her. If that wasn't enough, Edward's love of Bella and need to protect her has led him to kill another vampire. This threatens Bella because other vampires now want to kill her in revenge.

Family Conflict

Bella's family situation also causes her some different kinds of conflict. She's had to adjust to a new family situation as her mother has remarried. Although her stepfather, a professional sportsman, is nice, Bella knows that it is not fair on her mother not to travel with him. So Bella experiences a loss of life with her mother by moving in with her father in Forks.

Community Conflict

The community of Forks is riddled with conflict. The "bad" vampires are killing humans, and the police are on the hunt for what they believe is a savage animal. This is a potential threat to Bella because if the truth were known, it could drive the Cullen family away from the area. There is also an ancient conflict between the vampire clan and a wolf clan in the same territory.

Culture Conflict

The main cultural clash in *Twilight* is between the world of humans and vampires. Humans are the natural prey of vampires. It takes huge self-restraint for the vampire family to be "vegetarian" by only feeding on the blood of animals.

Nation Conflict

By showing a very different version of ancient American mythology, the wider sense of territory and alternative national mythology is explored in the story.

World Conflict

Before Bella finds out that Edward is a vampire, she knows a great deal doesn't add up about him for a normal guy. Her secret investigations lead her to discover the mythological origins of vampires from all over the world. This gives a worldly dimension to the story.

Now let's turn to a very different kind of film, which explores internal antagonism.

The Milk of Sorrow

Internal Conflict

Fausta, the heroine, has been emotionally scarred by her mother Susi's personal tragedy. Raped by terrorists in the civil war when she was pregnant, Susi suffered almost unimaginable atrocity. She was forced to eat her murdered husband's penis. Susi has brought up her daughter to fear life and, in particular, all men. As a young woman, Fausta copes with the Maternal Lesson of fear of rape by keeping a potato as a stopper in her vagina, a superstitious form of protection.

Significant Other Conflict

Her mother's death presents Fausta with a huge problem. She wants to give Susi a proper burial in the graveyard, not just a hole in her uncle's back garden. However, she is very poor and cannot do this. Not only does she have to cope with the loss of her mother, but also she has to embalm Susi's body and keep it hidden in the uncle's house. Later on, her rich female boss and the friendly male gardener become alternative "significant others" to Fausta. The gardener in particular is sensitive and understands her syndrome, but she is too damaged to cope with being understood by a man and gets angry with him. Her boss makes a deal with Fausta to sing, and in return she will give Fauasta pearls that she can then sell to pay for the burial. Eventually, the boss sacks Fausta, reneging on the deal. Fausta has to deal with her Internal Conflict — her fears — to take action to solve all her problems.

Family Conflict

Fausta's uncle does not want the body of the mother in the house, as preparations for his own daughter's wedding proceed. He gives her a deadline by which time her mother must be gone from the house, or he will bury her in the garden. Fausta is very much a second-class citizen in the family.

Community Conflict

The local community is a fearful place for Fausta. She is terrified of walking alone and receiving attention from young men. Superstitions are rife in the local community, which also generates a layer of conflict for Fausta. She believes them, and her life is thus restricted by them.

Culture Conflict

The superstitious values of the old women like Susi hold their daughters back from living fully and freely.

Nation Conflict

Peru's civil insurrection caused a huge internal split between the people. The horrific atrocities and indignities both sides inflicted on each other have left lasting scars. These permeate the story.

World Conflict

Peru is a developing country in the world. The poverty and political tensions give a global scale to the film.

Tip for Writing the Layers of Conflict

If you can get your scenes or sequences to reflect as many layers of conflict as possible, your story will be very powerful. For an example of how well this can be done, watch *4 Months, 3 Weeks and 2 Days*. In one hotel room, every single layer of conflict is somehow represented, from the World (isolated Romania in the 1980s with its extreme reproduction policies) down to the Internal Conflict, as heroine Otilia has to choose between having sex against her wishes and forcing her friend to accept the consequences of an unwanted pregnancy.

PSYCHODYNAMICS AND CONFLICT

How your heroine emotionally copes with conflict will very much depend on her particular psychology. Knowing some basic principles about the psychodynamics of conflict can really help you know your heroine inside out. You don't need to be an expert in psychoanalysis to work with these, of course. It's not as if you are giving your character therapy and she might sue you for being unqualified! But when it comes to writing scenes, an understanding of psychodynamics will certainly add an extra layer of depth.

What do I mean by psychodynamics of conflict? These are unconscious internal processes, which are ways the character has developed to deal with life. Understanding them will help you know how your heroine reacts or deals with all the layers of conflict. It's important to remember that your character might experience each of these psychodynamics at different stages in the story. Different situations might provoke different reactions. However, we all have some fundamental ways of coping with emotions, learnt from childhood. Because they help us survive, they aren't all bad either. But taken to extremes, they can be very destructive to oneself and relationships. It takes a great deal of healing and self-awareness to change these deeply rooted patterns.

The psychodynamics that are really helpful in developing characters' interactions are:

∞ Projection

∞ Denial

∞ Repression

∞ Fantasy

Projection — All about Self-Protection

Very often we blame or accuse others of having bad qualities or traits that we have ourselves. This is projection. Projection basically protects us from self-criticism. It helps us survive the horror of being ourselves and our dark sides! People who project a great deal can be very frustrating for others to be around because they have a lack of self-truth, and they find it difficult to see their part in a situation. They can be very manipulative. Or they are simply very scared. Normally they project a great deal because they don't have high self-esteem or much self-awareness. Not all accusations are projection, however. Sometimes a heroine might be making a really good point about another character's limitations or an unfair situation. This is why projection is a complex dynamic for women in a world that still isn't equal. It's easy for a woman to find fault with what's holding her back, but sometimes she can get stuck in blaming everything else because she is angry with her own lack of ability to take action. Genuine powerlessness is a terrible thing, and it still can exist for women in the West, but very often women can feel like victims because they don't want to pay the high price of walking away.

This sense of unfairness can play itself out in intimate relation-ships. Women frequently feel like the victims in a relationship, because they can feel burdened with children and housework. It's easier to blame others for a situation that your heroine might be colluding with in some way. It's doubly confusing when cultural expectations (such as being a stay-at-home mom) encourage a woman to live life in a certain way that doesn't suit her or bring her happiness. This double bind might make her lash out in anger.

Your heroine might unconsciously be carrying around some emotional wounds from the past. Her way of dealing with these might be to project all those aspects of herself onto other people. However, it's important to remember that if your heroine is projecting, then she's learnt to do this for a reason. It's your job to work out why. This is how the psychodynamic of projection can play out for your heroine:

Your heroine projects:

∞ Self-hate as a belief that somebody else hates her.

∞ Anger as an accusation that others are angry.

∞ Self-pity as a conviction that others are victimizing her.

∞ Selfishness as a belief everyone else is selfish.

Famous heroines who project are Terry Ann in *The Upside of Anger* who rants and raves about how bad her husband is after he disappears, Andrea in *The Devil Wears Prada*, when she thinks that her friends and boyfriend aren't supportive to her work, and Carrie in *Sex and the City* who projects her inability to commit onto men.

Denial — All about the Power

Are women more self-reflective? No! Denial, like all psychodynamic processes, affects men and women equally. Because women tend to find it easier to share emotions, they might get more opportunity for realizing that they are denying, but a good woman denier can equal her male counterpart any day. Deniers deny as a defense mechanism in order to maintain control and power to hide deep feelings of anxiety. It is a need to be thought of as strong so others can't hurt you. It's not so much about putting on a mask; it's about really believing that the best face to show yourself and others is a strong one. People who deny bad stuff are generally quite good at getting ahead, and can be positive thinkers. This is a good quality. "You are your thoughts" is a basic principle of self-awareness, and deniers can often prove that positive thinking is the way to go. However, there is a destructive side to denying. People who deny a great deal aren't the most empathetic people. They don't want to get their hands dirty with other people's pain or misery. They don't mind power, but responsibility isn't really their thing. And too much denial can mean that the individual can fall apart in a real crisis. Research has proven that gloomy people make better decisions in life because seeing the downside means you can evaluate risk better. If you are a denier, you could be disputing this very fact now!

Women who deny can often be feisty, fun-loving, and into the good life. They expect loyalty, have a regal bearing, and hate gossip or gloomy talk. Deniers tend to be loners or fiercely independent beings who have come through hardship or got where they are through their own efforts without much support.

A heroine who denies might say:

- ∞ "I'm not angry" to really mean "you want to bug me but you can't."
- ∞ "I'm not jealous" to really mean "I'm not going to show you I'm hurt."

∞ "It's not so bad" to really mean "don't bring me down."

Some famous heroines who deny are Scarlett O'Hara in *Gone with the Wind*, who refuses to see defeat in any area of her life, Samantha in *Sex and the City*, who lives for self-pleasure, Amanda Woods in *The Holiday*, who doesn't want to see what she's doing wrong in relationships, and Maggie, the younger sister in *In Her Shoes*, who refuses to see her envy of her cleverer sister Rose.

Repression — All about Fear

Women who repress their true emotions have generally been taught that their feelings are not worthy of consideration or important enough. They can have terrible low self-esteem or have been damaged by abusive situations that they weren't helped through sufficiently. For these women, repression is a safer bet than facing or reliving the emotional trauma. It's a bit like a scar that has healed over, leaving some infection behind. The pain is always there, but sometimes it's not so obvious. A repressing woman usually develops elaborate ways of hiding her scars and thinks she's convinced everyone they aren't there, when the signs are really obvious to the people who are close to her. Repressed emotions can manifest as passivity, which can be frustrating for others. If a fairly well-adjusted woman suffers a violating trauma in adult life (such as torture, violence, or rape) she might repress even if this goes against her natural openness because trauma is usually accompanied by shock. If a woman has no one to trust, or comes from a culture that doesn't permit communication with strangers, then she might not get the professional support she needs.

A heroine who represses might be scarred by:

∞ Low self-esteem and shows it by being dependent, with no autonomy, or through passive behavior.

∞ Humiliation and shows it by self-mutilation, eating disorders.

∞ Sexual abuse and shows it by false sexuality, pleasing others.

∞ Loss and shows it by anger, guilt, or exhaustion.

∞ Trauma and shows it by withdrawal, numbness, insecurity.

Memorable heroines who repress are Rachel in *Rachel Getting Married*, Precious in *Precious*, and Juliette in *I've Loved You So Long*.

Fantasy — All about Escapism

Fantasy and the power of our imagination make life a better place. It's why we read stories, watch movies and plays, and have dreams and become writers. To be a visionary, to make change in the world, you have to be able to see a better reality and believe it can happen. It's a wonderful gift of humanity. Fantasists are people who have a powerful need to escape reality as a coping mechanism. Sometimes a fantasy helps us bear a nightmare reality. Sometimes a fantasy becomes real. Loving someone who doesn't love us back sometimes does lead to them changing their minds. Conviction is convincing, after all. But too much fantasy can be destructive. The rise in virtual reality online games such as avatar-run worlds is a reflection on the large number of fantasists out there, people who, for whatever reason, need to spend many hours of their life being anywhere but the here and now. In *Avatar*, the Hero Jake finds a better 'real' life through his avatar self. Fantasy life might be a coping mechanism for extreme feelings of inadequacy, or simply boredom and depression-induced inertia. Emotional literacy tends to be a very low factor in the extreme fantasist. Fantasizing can take many forms of behavior, such as sexual fantasy, addictions from drug taking to compulsive reading, and pathological lying. Someone who idealizes others a great deal might have a tendency to fantasize. They prefer a vision of reality rather than the real thing. A criminal fantasist is someone who drags other people into their dark reality.

If your heroine fantasizes she can believe:

∞ She should be with a man when reality says he's not interested.

∞ She can fulfill her ambitions when reality says the odds are against her.

∞ She has a fairy godmother when reality demonstrates her family hates her (Precious).

∞ Passion can last forever when reality says love has ups and downs.

Examples of heroines who need to fantasize are Edith Piaf in *La Vie en Rose*, who uses drugs to help with her fragile grasp on life, Cristina in *Vicky Cristina Barcelona*, who has a fear of mundane relationships, and Ofelia in *Pan's Labyrinth*, who enters another world to cope with Franco's brutal regime in Spain and her difficult family life.

EXERCISE: YOUR HEROINE'S CONFLICT QUESTIONNAIRE

First, brainstorm all the layers of conflict in your story. This will trigger some great insights. It doesn't matter if you aren't quite sure yet but try to identify how all the layers might be symbolized in the story. The process will help you decide which layers of conflict are more important for you to focus on. Then, imagining you are in the shoes of your heroine, complete Your Heroine's Conflict Questionnaire.

YOUR HEROINE'S CONFLICT QUESTIONNAIRE

1. Who or what is your biggest problem? Why?

2. What gets in the way of you living your life exactly how you want?

3. Who or what do you dislike in your family?

4. How do you feel about how other family members treat you?

5. What is your deepest cause of unhappiness?

6. What can you do about this?

7. Who takes up most of your thoughts? Why do they?

8. What are the main causes of problems in your closest relationships?

9. What are your problems at work? How can you change these?

10. If you could turn back the clock in any area of your life to do things differently, what would it be? How would you change things?

FEELING GOOD
AND FINDING LOVE

Chapter 7

The flipside of conflict is union. Union can mean joy, peace, and harmony. It can also mean the coming together of two people, or a group of people, who feel truly connected with each other. Union essentially means being at one. It is the deepest human need, yet one that takes a myriad of forms in our stories.

THE IMPORTANCE OF UNION

So why is it that as a dramatic principle union is so overwhelmingly overlooked? Read most of the screenwriting books, and the mantra are conflict, conflict, conflict, or, obstacles, tests, and challenges. From Aristotle to today's screenwriting gurus, no conflict equals no story. The bottom line is that the focus on conflict negates other equally important human needs. Linda Seger makes this point in *When Women Call the Shots* (1996). She asked many women filmmakers (writers, directors, and producers) how they felt their stories were different from men's. Harmony was a big issue for many of these women.

Harmony is central to female identity, and that's one of the reasons it has been ignored by dramatists. The ability to let a baby grow in your own body and feel good about it is the deepest source of union. Nurturing a child, whether it is breast-feeding, nappy changing, reading a bedtime story, and constantly needing to see life with two sets of eyes, is being in a state of union with another. Why masculine theories about story have undermined union might be because up until fairly recently gender roles have traditionally excluded men from the hands-on side of caring and nurturing others.

Masculine identity deals out different kinds of conflict for men to handle. Protector and provider roles are easier to manage if a man has power and control. Whether its money, social standing, or employment, a man is defined by what he does. Achieving status is a lonely battle, fraught with competition and rivalry. Seeking union is something the male psyche needs but doesn't easily allow itself as it is associated with women and "femininity."

You might believe women are naturally better at relationships, and that women are the ones who promote bonds and provide the nurturing. Some feminists would say that women haven't really had much choice but to marry well and become nurturers, until they fought for independence and equal rights. The vast numbers of women today who achieve and want external success backs this up. Evolutionists would say that women's need to have babies to keep the human tribe going makes them want stories about finding and keeping love. Others, including me, would say that men and women have exactly the same needs for union in the form of love, harmony, peace, and joy.

Conflict is important. It's vital to storytelling. I'm saying it's time to elevate the principle of union to its rightful place in the dramatic tradition. Let's also start saying *no union, no story*! Whether your favorite recent film is *Mamma Mia!* or *Precious*, these stories wouldn't have their wide appeal without union.

CULTURAL UNION

Joy, happiness, peace, and love are the upsides of caring for others, being a part of a family and community. We need love to thrive. Women, at least in the West, are the overt joy makers and seekers. *Sex and the City* put the highs and more highs of female friendship firmly on the map. Countless romantic comedies show heroines leading stories in which love for a man is the main deal. *Julie and Julia* oozes with the pleasures of joy, food, love, and sex. Even darker stories like *My Summer of Love* which spends half the story exploring the delights of the unrestrained female friendship of two teenage girls. The almost obligatory wedding scene at the end of the romantic comedy is an acceptable cliché we smile at.

How women can express their joy in one culture will vary hugely from another culture. Probably the most joyless cultures for women are those that remove girls' clitorises. To deny a woman the source of sexual pleasure is rooted in an almost incomprehensible fear and a need to control. Can you imagine a culture in which women subject men to such an extent that men perform castration on each other, and tell each other it's for their own good? It sounds like a bad "B" movie by a psychotic female Tarantino. In extremely male-dominated culture, stories with heroines don't tend to be too upbeat. Moments of union, if any, are snatched away and constantly under threat. Heroines have to tow the line and woe betides them if they rebel. *Whale Rider's* heroine takes a whole film to prove herself to the tribal elders. The women in *At Five in the Afternoon* rarely show defiance, and when they do, it's momentary and angst ridden. Freedom definitely equates the ability to have fun.

I spent many years working in Romania. I visited many orphanages and saw firsthand the failure of babies to thrive in institutional care. The national tragedy has left a scar on the people. It's not a co-incidence that the family problems are a metaphoric wound in many contemporary films coming out of Romania now. These are not joyful stories. They are stories about the struggle of the family unit. They are stories about a culture trying to heal the wound of the people.

MEN AND UNION

As men take on more roles that were once seen as traditionally feminine, it's no coincidence that their stories show more aspects of union. Expressions of joy are seen less as women's emotional stuff and as more "human." Bollywood has a head start where men express love, passion, and dance; the U.S. has the bromance and bromedy in which the male friendship is celebrated. And the U.K.? Well, we still have repressed Mark Darcy but even he is loosening up. It seems that men have cottoned on to the fact that they are depriving themselves of the sheer bliss of caring, sharing, and loving — each other. At last they are giving themselves permission to express joy, happiness, and the beauty of friendship. Competitive sports, the objectification of women, and the thrill of winning and getting the girl are still visible in some overtly masculine stories, but things are changing. My main gripe with the bromance is that the male protestations of love for each other still manage to negate the female characters and make them feel slightly alien and subordinate to the male friendship. *Pineapple Express* and *I Love You, Man* are good examples of this syndrome. How many girl buddy films do you see in which the man is marginalized at the altar while the two women friends declare undying love?

UNION AND YOUR HEROINE'S' STORY

The principle of union is extremely important to many heroines' stories and women-orientated genres. It can sometimes seem like an overriding principle. It's true that many women like stories that explore love, even if it's love gone wrong. Women seem to prefer emotional stories in which the heroine experiences relationships, including the highs and lows of happiness, loss, caring, warmth, intimacy, and commitment — the joyful aspect of being in a family or a relationship.

How you personally feel about the joyous and union-filled aspects of heroines' stories will very much depend on your own attitudes to union. For instance, if you are a man who recoils at overt joyous femininity, you might feel very uncomfortable around emotions and label them women's stuff. This is where "chick lit" and "chick flicks" have emerged from, a strong need to label anything about relationships as women's light and fluffy stuff. The more open you are to expressions of emotion, the more you might enjoy stories about love and friendship. You might like films such as *Sideways* and *A Single Man* because they show men experiencing deeply emotional situations, by following the Path to Wholeness story type.

If you are a woman who basically identifies with the relatively gender-free Future Femininity Supertheme, you might cringe at films like *Mamma Mia!* The overlayering of union in genres such as romantic comedies and comedies might be off-putting to you. Or you might prefer more "masculine" action-oriented movies. Many women writers love union as much as women audiences. You want to create stories that reflect joy, harmony, happiness, and love. The Layers of Union can help you do this.

THE LAYERS OF UNION

Just like you need to work out the layers of conflict in your heroine's story, you need to know the layers of union. They directly correspond to the layers of conflict. The layers of union are:

∞ Layer 1: Internal Union

∞ Layer 2: Significant Other Union

∞ Layer 3: Family Union

∞ Layer 4: Community Union

∞ Layer 5: Culture Union

∞ Layer 6: Nation Union

∞ Layer 7: World Union

Layer 1: Internal Union

Internal union is a sense of inner peace, self-acceptance, and contentment. It's a state of mind that is free from anxiety, self-doubts, negative thoughts, and destructive emotions. In many ways, inner peace is connected to an ability to feel part of the whole, an ability to see ourselves as one, not as a separate from everyone else. It's a transcendental way of being. This internal state of grace can be very difficult for humans, with our demanding egos and our need to compete, survive, and achieve.

Internal union has many different facets for women. Women experience an overwhelming number of thoughts each day about their self-image. This comes from culture judging women on how they look and women buying into this judgment and doesn't exactly lend itself to a transcendental way of thinking. For some women, self-image anxiety is permanently on the back of their mind, to the point of obsession. Rare and fortunate is the woman who feels great about herself. Even rarer is the heroine who gives off self-assured contentment about her self-image (and it isn't a problem in the story).

Pregnancy is a physical state of internal union. Not only is a woman creating life inside her body, that life is part of her and growing from her. Other parts of her body, like her immune system, will shut down to protect the life in the womb. Pregnant women can experience a very powerful form of union with their unborn child. They are literally fused with another.

It's possible that as a woman ages, and finds herself increasingly invisible, she might be able to achieve self-acceptance that isn't dependent on approval of her looks. I'm sure that if you are a woman reading this, you will have had the same thoughts. Thoughts along the lines of... "When I'm old and ugly, I won't even care anymore!"

Self-union also takes the form of masturbation. A woman who feels at one with herself can give herself pleasure in a very satisfying way. Many women find it extremely difficult to feel comfortable with their own bodies, as sex education doesn't tend to teach girls about understanding their own feelings of desire and emphasizes the risks of penetration. The true organ of pleasure for a woman is the clitoris, championed most overtly by *Sex and the City* and the rise of the Rampant Rabbit vibrator but rarely in love-making scenes. In *The Private Lives of Pippa Lee*, Pippa has nonpenetrative sex with her neighbor's son. He is a spiritually minded man, and his way of making love to her can be seen as an act of giving to a woman who is not good at putting herself first.

Layer 2: Significant Other

This layer is all about the sense of union we get from another individual. It's the governing principle behind the desire for love and intimacy. It symbolizes our need to find our soul mate, friend for life, and fellow traveler. Union also reflects the earliest memories of oneness we all felt with our first caretakers, even the safety of the womb. Union, at its most primal, is a dependent and unconditional bond. Love with a significant other, whether it's a lover, child, or parent, can be blissful. It's nice to be completely understood and to understand the other.

Women's desire for love is not necessarily stronger than men's, but it does tend to dominate many heroines' stories. Women are able to express this desire more because, as I've mentioned, it's that much more permissible in our culture.

The romantic ideal of man as savior is very powerful, but it tends to be an empty myth for women who have very close early relationships with their mothers and fathers. These women have strong self-esteem and idealization of the other is not such a factor for them. These women seek equal relationships and the need to be saved is not such a feature of their love. But how many women have this? Most of us have been brought up by mothers, stressed, tired, loving, and supportive in equal measure. She's the figure we love and we hate in equal measure. If finding love is important to your heroine, it's a good idea to really know her backstory. What is getting in the way of her ability to find love with the right person? What wounds does she have to heal to be able to love?

In love relationships, the physical act of sex is an intensely powerful union, when it's between two people who really care for each other. Sex that is not based on intimacy tends to be fuelled by eroticism and fantasy projections about the other person. The sense of arousal is not dependent on knowing the person deeply and doesn't have the sense of intimacy that comes from commitment, trust, and openness. This is why you can have bad sex with the person you are committed to when trust issues, power dynamics, and lack of communication are sabotaging the relationship. What kind of sex life does your heroine have? Think about how she feels pleasure, and whether intimacy is easy for her.

Layer 3: Family

Birthdays, weddings, anniversaries, and even funerals where we share our deepest memories of the loved one, and bade them farewell, symbolize the union in family life. A family can give a sense of belonging and connection that is truly special and everlasting. Again, the biological family might not be as important as those your heroine believes make up her real family — the people around her who really care for her. It's important for you to work out whether the family really offers your heroine a sense of union, and how.

Female friends and women's support networks become like family to many women. Women's ability to share and empathize with each other is equalized by an ability to care for each other. The notion of sisterhood is built on the understanding that women understand the burdens placed on each other and are the best people to really share the load. *The Virgin Suicides* is a mysterious exploration of sisterly love that achieves a state of ultimate union through death.

Layer 4: Community

Union in the community is symbolized in the all the ways a community looks out for each other, celebrates together, and supports each other. Your heroine will always be in a community of one sort or another, so how is she going to experience union there? In *St. Trinian's*, the community of renegade and anarchic British boarding school girls is also their family (most of them being dumped their by rejecting families). Union comes in the form of riotous pranks and a live and let live philosophy.

Layer 5: Culture

Expressions of union are shaped and determined by a heroine's culture. In the course of your research, you might find some surprising aspects of cultural union. In my research for a screenplay set in the Edwardian era, I discovered that weekend house parties were all the rage for the aristocrats. In addition to the hunting, feasting, and dancing there would be spouse swapping. A servant would ring a discreet bell at 6 a.m. so that philandering partners could creep back into their rightful beds to join their spouses! This happened up and down the country in all the aristocratic houses. Whatever her culture, there will be a whole variety of ways expression of union are permitted. The more male-dominated a culture is, joy for women can be furtive, often taking place in and among women.

Layer 6: Nation

A nation's sense of union is often seen in stories in which success or achievement is celebrated. This could be victory or another kind of commemoration of a nation's pride. Dedication is a strong drive in the heroine who wants to make her country proud or to fight for it in some way, even if it is simply by supporting her husband going to war. National heroines can be sportswomen, such as the heroine in *National Velvet* and *International Velvet*. The truly heroic heroine who is not scared to put down her life is primarily motivated for the common good. If she survives, her victory is a shared one. Many women aren't recognized for their achievements until after their deaths and remain forgotten heroines. Writing a film about their lives in order to share it with the world is a form of belated celebration. *Rabbit-Proof Fence* celebrates the bravery of female aboriginal children.

Layer 7: World

This is symbolized by the fragile notion of world peace. It comes from alliance and diplomatic efforts to sustain good relations between countries. Women as politicians are taking their place on the world stage, yet there are still too few of them. The Olympics represent the union of nations in sports. Although the action is competitive, the spirit of cooperation is the overriding principle. Women athletes and politicians extend women's participation on the world stage. Let's take a look at the layers of union in two very different films, *Mamma Mia!* and *The Secret Life of Bees.*

Mamma Mia!

Mamma Mia! is a global phenomenon that filled movie theaters all over the world with female audiences who saw the film many times, many of whom have never seen the musical version on stage. Was it just the Abba songs that made it so extraordinarily successful? They certainly helped the exuberance of the production, but the film's utter joyousness, its celebration of love and life, of mother/daughter relationships, female bonding, and the power of love were other equally important ingredients in the recipe of success. It's easy to laugh at *Mamma Mia!* but not at the box-office numbers. It was a resounding commercial success. So why did the film have such a powerful connection with women (and men who don't have a problem with Feel Good Femininity!)? I am sure the success of the film was due to the rich layers of union that took precedence over the conflict, jeopardy, and stakes.

Layer 1: Internal Union

The joint heroines of *Mamma Mia!* are Sophie, a young woman on the verge of getting married, and her mother Donna. Sophie is a character with a great sense of fun and is expressive and vital. The love and support she's had from Donna as a mother has given Sophie strong self-esteem reflected in her ability to fall for the right guy. Donna has less internal union than Sophie because of baggage from the past, but she's still got a fair degree of inner strength and harmony. She's got a sense of pride in her work achievements, is proud of her daughter, and like Sophie, still has the capacity to have a good time.

Layer 2: Significant Other Union

Sophie's love for both her fiancé Skye and her mother Donna are great sources of happiness for her. Her relationship with Skye is full of sexual passion. He cares, understands, and wants the best for her, and is her equal in showing affection and emotion. He is also a loyal guy who will neglect his own needs to be by her side. Sophie's love for Donna is slightly more complex, but she is devoted to her mother and grateful for all she has done for her.

Donna adores her daughter so much she doesn't want her to leave the island. For many single mothers, their whole identity depends on their role as mother. This is the case for Donna who wants to be the mother for Sophie that she never had herself – supportive, encouraging, and close. The other significant other in Donna's life is Sam, who comes back for Sophie's wedding. He was the big love of her life before a mis-understanding drove them apart. Happiness for Donna comes at the end of the film when Sam gets down on bended knee and proposes. He has always loved her, always loved the island, and wants to spend the rest of his life with her. Not only that, he also understands she needs to let go of Sophie. What choice does Donna have but to say "I do!" to a guy who understands her so completely?

For mother and daughter, happiness from significant others comes from being honest, being real, and letting someone else in.

Layer 3: Family Union

Sophie and Donna's family love not only comes from their intense mother/daughter relationship, but also the wider family each of them have. They both have two special girlfriends who are like sis-ters to them. Sophie even refers to her mother's friends as "aunties." These sisterly friends know Donna and Sophie backward. They are close, loving confidants and partners in the crime of having as much raucous fun as possible.

Layer 4: Community Union

The Greek island is a loving community where overworked Greek women can throw down their aprons and become dancing queens. They love and support Donna, and work hard for her. The island is beautiful, verdant, and surrounded by a magical azure sea. It's hard to imagine anything really bad happening here, and in the story, it doesn't!

Layer 5: Culture Union

The ancient symbol of love in the form of Aphrodite's Fountain gives the story a mythical dimension.

Layer 6: Nation Union

Greece is seen as a warm and caring nation in the story. It's a country where different people live happily side by side and nothing threatening happens. It's a country people travel to so they can escape their lives.

Layer 7: World Union

The wider world beyond the island is also a positive factor in *Mamma Mia!* for both heroines. Sophie ends up traveling the world with Skye, having resolved her Maternal Lessons and Father Distance issues. She's now going to have the wild fun life that her once nomadic mother had. Donna's past life revisits her in the form of her three international boyfriends, and their arrival on the island heals all the unresolved issues of her life. You get a sense Donna's reunion with Sam is going to give her a more international life again.

Now let's move on to a film in which union is just as important but takes place in a completely different setting and time.

The Secret Life of Bees

Layer 1: Internal Union

Although Lily has painful emotional wounds from losing her mother when she was three, she also manages to experience a sense of internal union in a fantasy of her life with her mother. She also has the gift of writing, which reflects an ability to enjoy the company of one's own thoughts. By the end of the story she is at peace with herself and enjoying her life.

Layer 2: Significant Other Union

Lily has a deep love of her nanny Rosaleen, by whom she feels protected and cared for. She forms a deep relationship with August, who was her mother's nanny. August is warm, understanding, and able to meet Lily's emotional wounds. Eventually, Lily forms a special bond with Zach, a boy her age. They feel romantically attached to each other and encourage each other to share their dreams. He is the first positive male role model for Lily, who has been brutalized by her father.

Layer 3: Family Union

By entering the Boatwright sisters' household, Lily finally achieves a sense of belonging. The sisters have created a special and safe environment where racism and hostility are shut out. A misfit at first, all the sisters grow to love her in different ways. The last one to love her is June. When Lily sprays her with water, June's icy reserve finally melts. Not only does she play with Lily and the others in the water fight, she lets herself cry in front of Lily and be comforted by her. As Lily proudly says herself at the end of her story, "I have three mothers."

Layer 4: Community Union

Although the Deep South is riddled with racism, the sisters have managed to create a sense of love in their own community. The white lawyer respects and supports them.

Layer 5: Culture Union

The power of the black Madonna statuette in the household symbolizes the hope and strength of African Americans.

Layer 6: Nation Union

National politics, the Civil Rights Act, and desegregation all reflect a nation taking the right steps toward uniting the people and aspiring to treat all as equals.

Layer 7: World Union

The roots of Africa are symbolized in the story as the proud heritage of the African American community. This gives a global dimension to the otherwise very localized story.

THE STEPS TO LOVE

Most screenwriting guides don't pay much attention to the process of falling in love. When you consider the number of heroines' stories that have a relationship at their heart, it can be useful to have a model that helps you think through the dynamics of finding love and experiencing a relationship.

The model I'm going to present to you is a result of many factors; my own experiences of life and love, writing about relationships, and watching films about relationships. Just like the phases of a heroine's story, these steps are not necessarily linear. Relationships are organic, constantly in flux, and sensitive to many internal and external factors. Many of these steps are truly repetitive as well. Although a couple is making progress, they might repeat certain steps. A couple may go through the cycle and back to the beginning again. Or one person in the relationship might go back to earlier steps or even jump ahead. This is commonly felt in relationships that feel out of balance, when one person isn't ready, and feels the other is pushing too much.

So as you get to know the steps to love, just like the story phases I presented earlier, you'll be able to use them to build the story you want to tell. The steps to love are completely complementary to the phases. One set doesn't replace another, and you can pick and choose to suit the needs of your story. In love, we can stand on one step for a very long time. Or we can hop, skip, and jump, in any order we feel like! Love is never a linear process.

Different films and genres reflect some of the steps and not others. It's usual that romantic comedies start with the first stage of "Rules of Attraction" and end with "Taking the Plunge," when the couple gets married. But increasingly, heroines' stories follow what happens after a marriage, divorce, or the dating game when you've got children or other complications. The steps are no longer straightforward, because love never is. It is very common for a heroine's love story to focus on the way love relationships affect a character's sense of identity. You can also follow the steps to love in nonsexual relationships, which are about two people who have a very close bond.

∾ Step 1: The Void

∾ Step 2: Running Scared

∾ Step 3: Feeling the Fear

∾ Step 4: Killing Illusion

∾ Step 5: Baring the Soul

∾ Step 6: The Plunge

∾ Step 7: Test of Trust

∾ Step 8: The Lost Self

∾ Step 9: Renegotiation

∾ Step 10: Acceptance

Step 1: The Void

Before a new relationship starts, there is usually some kind of void in a heroine's life. She may be single or unhappily married. She may have no need for a relationship, or she may crave one. She might have created a protective bubble around her, or she might be on a dating frenzy. She might have survived the loss of a previous partner or other loved one. She might have stumbled into a professional relationship with the potential lover. If she's Bridget Jones in *Bridget Jones's Diary*, she will feel she is gathering dust on the shelf, another unwanted thirty-something singleton. At the end of *The Hours*, Virginia Woolf enters the Void of death. The step of Acceptance (see following text) leads her to the conclusion that suicide is the only right thing to do for herself and Leonard, her husband.

Step 2: Running Scared

The heroine meets the potential lover and she… runs scared! This is metaphoric, remember. She's not necessarily tearing off down the street. Attraction can be conscious or deeply unconscious, depending on where she is at in her life and what she is telling herself. She will normally trust her own intuition as well as her own projections about this potential lover before her, even if she hasn't consciously realized they could be a lover. He or she might be exactly what she is looking for, or she might reel in horror at their odious traits. She might not feel she is ready and retreat. If she is desperate to love, she might be fearful that her new or potential lover might cause hurt or disappointment. He might not be interested, she might not be good enough, or he might be the same old bad type she is always attracted to. Unconscious feelings of inadequacy can dominate this time, when good and bad fantasies about the other person fill the mind. Defenses are huge and designed to protect both individuals. You can see this in countless romantic comedies in which both characters loath the very aspects that they are not only misreading, but that they will come to accept and heal in each other. This reflects the dynamics of projection in which another person reminds us about the parts of ourselves we don't like but can't face up to.

One thing is for sure, whatever information a heroine is telling herself about the other person, the last thing she knows is the truth about her potential lover. This can only be discovered by getting involved. Remember, the potential lover is also going through exactly the same kind of anxieties. Many relationships don't get to first base because one or the other takes off. A worse-case scenario is that a commitment, for whatever reason, is formed when the character is Running Scared. This could be because of an arranged marriage, or a heroine choosing to marry as a form of escape or because she has no other choice, like Ada in *The Piano* and Kitty in *The Painted Veil*. In *The Proposal*, Andrew is stuck with his boss Margaret because she has trapped him into marrying her.

Step 3: Feeling the Fear

A deeper level of connection is achieved by new information or a revelation about the potential lover coming to light. He might ask her on a date. She might ask him on a date. A heroine might have a one-night stand with the potential lover, and they could talk more openly afterward. There is a shift in perception about the other person, leading to both parties feeling a risk of getting closer is worth taking. The unconscious dynamic behind this stage is that something about the other person reminds the heroine of herself, leading to a glimmer of empathy. The projections are still there, as the heroine is still largely defining the potential lover by her own experiences and assumptions. By opening the door slightly wider, the potential lover is let in. Each partner feels the risk of proceeding is worth taking, even if it doesn't end up well and help the relationship go forward. In *The Proposal*, Margaret lies in bed and tells Andrew about her emotional scars from her parents' death. Andrew now has some understanding why her defenses, which make her a controlling and unlikeable boss, are so massive. He can start to see her in a different light.

Step 4: Killing Illusion

If things do go well, the heroine wants to know everything about the lover. She feels deeply attracted and wants to make sure she's making the right decisions. She will feel more secure the more she knows. Illusion only gets in the way. Depending on the intentions of the lover, he or she will feel the same. A deeper connection can grow from both lovers letting the mask down. Depending how safe each person feels, the more truth they will reveal. Killing Illusion also involves facing up to self-delusion. In *Bridget Jones: The Edge of Reason*, many of Bridget's paranoid delusions are shattered as she learns the truth about Mark. The defenses that the heroine has built up around her are exposed as a means of keeping others out. The loved one's baggage is recognized and accepted and is not seen as a deterrent. Mutual opening up and surprising revelations can take place. Sometimes Killing Illusion does result in Running Scared, by opening up a character can't handle the truth. This can lead to a deep sense of betrayal in the other person, especially if sex has occurred. Killing Illusion can also take place during a separation. It reflects a deep need to know and to make sense.

Step 5: Baring the Soul

Because Killing Illusion may have led to a relationship unfolding, an even deeper layer of intimacy is achieved. In stories, it is very common that Baring the Soul happens after a Test of Trust (see following text), when one or other of the partners feels betrayed by the other. To save the relationship, the other has to put herself on the line and finally expose her vulnerability. Ideally, Baring the Soul leads to a true sense of intimacy that balances the relationship and makes both partners equal. It will lead to reciprocal trust and love. However, it's not impossible for a deeply damaged person to require the other to Bare the Soul first to make them feel safe.

Baring the Soul is about reciprocity. It's the deepest form of transaction between two people. It's far more than just sex. The heroine now knows that her lover has the potential to heal her, and vice versa. He or she has all the necessary qualities to make the heroine feel whole. Their love is complementary and healing. The feeling they are made for each other takes over at this stage. Feeling safe, the heroine faces up to her deepest own inadequacies and projections. She feels an overwhelming need for her partner to know everything about her. She declares her deepest feelings and most private secrets and puts herself on the line for love. She tells the lover how she feels about him and what she wants. This can result in passionate lovemaking as a form of communication, when both people physically open up to each other.

Baring the Soul frequently occurs toward the end of numerous romantic comedies, sometimes as the end of an act 2 turning point when one character realizes how much damage she has caused the person she loves by not being truthful. In *The Proposal*, Margaret confesses not only to her lies but also to her feelings of love and respect for the people around her. It can also form the climax of act 3 in romances and romantic comedies.

Step 6: The Plunge

The couple commit to being together and taking their love seriously. For adults, it is often a marriage proposal. For teenagers, it is about getting serious and being seen as a couple by friends. A new era of love has arrived, and there is no turning back. Feelings of idealization about an unconditional love can rise here. The couple looks forward to a life together. This doesn't mean that ghosts from the past can't re-emerge here in the form of old wounds being pressed. The happy ending of many romantic comedies shows the Plunge being taken, for example the end of *What Happens in Vegas*. In *Thelma and Louise*, which portrays a nonsexual partnership, the women take a literal Plunge at the end, leading to the Void of Death.

Step 7: Test of Trust

The heroine and her lover's commitment is treasured or threatened here. A Test of Trust is the making of a spiritual commitment to one another. The Test of Trust can take the form of a wedding or a symbolic union of the new life. Alternatively it can be the betrayal of love, after Baring the Soul or The Plunge. In a tragic love story, the Test of Trust can result in the death or disappearance of the loved one. This can happen when the heroine is all alone. In *The English Patient*, Catherine lays dying, waiting for her lover to save her but he never comes back. She only has faith in him to make her last hours bearable. A sense of betrayal can also happen here, when an external factor exposes a past secret. In this case, the heroine can have total faith in her lover, or she can feel that only she properly Bared the Soul. *My Summer of Love* shows the shock the heroine feels when she discovers her best friend is not who she says she is. She has been fantasizing and lying about everything.

Step 8: The Lost Self

The committed relationship requires new compromises that all the stages up until the Plunge cannot fully prepare the couple for. It is as if, after the Test of Trust, the couple give birth to a new collective identity that must be nurtured as well as their own individual selves. If the Test of Trust is failed somehow, the heroine can feel lost and her identity shaken. She has to pick up the pieces of her shattered self and move on. She can eventually re-enter the Void. However, the Lost Self can also symbolize positive feelings in her heroine when she's lost sight of her true self, but she believes this isn't important. She's so in love, nothing else matters. Countless heroines' love stories focus on the huge change of identity that a relationship can bring about.

In *Two Days in Paris,* Marion experiences the Lost Self as she introduces her American boyfriend Jack to her French family, old Paris life, and old lovers and friends, and then has to deal with Jack's new perception of her. Most of the story focuses on the step of the Lost Self, leading to a breakdown in trust between her and Jack. Finally she has to Bare the Soul, leading to The Renegotiation.

Step 9: The Renegotiation

The committed relationship is disrupted or challenged by internal and external factors. The equilibrium is disturbed by major events, such as the birth of children, infertility, and job and financial challenges, that put pressure on the relationship and the nature of the union has to be renegotiated. Large-scale external factors such as war can threaten the love relationship. Internal needs and ambitions threaten the collective identity of the couple. One partner can feel left out or taken for granted. Old insecurities might resurface. Either partner has to go back to the steps of Killing Illusion or Baring the Soul to make the marriage or partnership survive; or it can be time to let the relationship die. For much of *Kramer vs. Kramer* the warring couple deal with the step of Renegotiation, as they battle over custody of their child. More recently, *The Break-Up* and *Brick Lane* are good examples of Renegotiation.

Step 10: Acceptance

The Renegotiation either results in a new form of union, which is tolerance and acceptance of the other's needs within the relationship, or of the couple finding a way of dealing with external factors so they don't damage the relationship. There is a sense of acceptance that feels durable, of the relationship having been made stronger by surviving the challenge. Alternatively, the relationship will die, and both partners will re-enter the Void or experience the Lost Self depending on how much the breakup affects them emotionally. In a long-term relationship, Acceptance can permeate the relationship on every level. Your heroine knows exactly how her partner ticks, and the compromise doesn't bother her. They have been through ups and down, trials and tribulations. Her partner is truly her other half.

The Steps to Love in Close-Up

Let's look at how the steps to love play out in *Sex and the City: The Movie*. This is an interesting example because the story charts the ongoing dynamics of intimacy after the supposed "happy ending" of the TV series, which in the case of Carrie and Big, happens in Paris at the end of Season 6 (as I'm sure fans of the series will remember all too well).

Sex and the City: The Movie

Carrie and Big prepare for their wedding day. Carrie is happy, feeling she is with Mr. Right. She's aware he's never written her a love letter, however. John (Big) is Running Scared of the wedding but hides it until it is too late. Carrie is preparing for the Plunge, planning her dream wedding, and getting sucked into the glitz and glamour of being in the public eye. When John finally asks for reassurance, needing to Kill the Illusion, Carrie can't get to her phone and doesn't get his messages. When the big day comes, John can't face the wedding. Jilted at the altar, or so she thinks, Carrie's Test of Trust is failed by John. Carrie (on the Retreat phase in which she lasts until the end of Act 2) experiences the Lost Self. She eventually realizes she has to Kill the Illusion, racking her brains to find out what she did wrong.

During this time, Carrie heals the Lost Self, by employing Louise, a personal assistant who is also experiencing the steps of love. Finally, Miranda confesses to Carrie that she warned John against marriage on the eve of the wedding. This new information instigates Carrie to Feel the Fear, and opens all the emails John sent her after the wedding. They are all love letters, in which he is Baring the Soul. Meeting at their abandoned apartment, Carrie and Big experience the Renegotiation, where now it is Carrie's turn to Bare the Soul. Acceptance of a new truthful relationship follows, based on truer communication and a better understanding of each other's needs, enabling them to Take the Plunge.

As for Miranda, her marriage has led her to the Lost Self. She is miserable, burnt out, and has gone off sex. She faces a Test of Love when Steve confesses he slept with someone else. Now, the Lost Self takes a turn for the worse. Becoming defiant, she enters the Void. Eventually, she and Steve end up at a counseling session. Miranda and Steve are both Running Scared at the thought of reuniting, but the counselling helps them Feel the Fear, leading to a Renegotiation. Their marriage now reaches the step of Acceptance.

Samantha also experiences the Lost Self for completely different reasons than Miranda. Her life in L.A. revolves around Jared, her young partner. She's not enjoying L.A., has put on loads of weight, and wants her old self back in Manhattan with her friends. Valentine's Night serves as a good Test of Love when she lies naked, covered in sushi. Jared is late, but it's the tipping point for Samantha. Renegotiation leads them to ending the relationship, which has a sense of Acceptance, with both remembering the good times with each other.

EXERCISE: YOUR HEROINE'S UNION QUESTIONNAIRE

First, brainstorm all the layers of union in your heroine's story. As with the layers of conflict, if you are unsure, don't worry. This exercise is designed to trigger new insights. Then, from your heroine's point of view, complete Your Heroine's Union Questionnaire. Finally, if you are writing a heroine's story in which an intimate relationship is explored, outline your story, identifying which steps to love function in your story.

YOUR HEROINE'S UNION QUESTIONNAIRE

1   What makes you happy? How do you show it?

2. Are you in love?

3. Describe all the emotional aspects of your relationship that bring you joy.

4. Do you have a good sex life? What fulfils you sexually?

5. What's the best thing about your family?

6. Who are your best friends? Why do you love them?

7. Would you describe your local community as a happy one? Why?

8. Do you have children? What's the best bit about parenting for you?

9. Who or what do you love most in the world?

10. What is your happiest memory?

GENRES FOR HEROINES' STORIES

Chapter 8

Finding the right genre for your heroine is a key to making her story memorable. This might seem something of a contradiction because if genre is anything, it's all about what makes a film able to be recognizable and categorized. You might also be thinking it is a bit late in the book to be having this discussion. Shouldn't we know the genre at the beginning of the process?

I don't think so. Sometimes we can get stuck to a preference for a particular genre because it is one we watch a great deal, we like, we are told is commercial, and will give our stories a better chance of getting made, or it is simply the one we know best. These might not actually serve your character and your story best. As you develop your heroine's character try to remain open to the fact that the genre might change. As most of your early stages will see you making huge transformations in character, plot, structure, and story, there's no reason why genre should be so preciously guarded.

When people ask you what you are working on, it's convenient to say "a love story" or "a psychological thriller." On the upside this helps it take form in your own mind, but the downside is that you might become overattached to a certain outcome. Sometimes, changing the genre can be the right solution to problems that have been ongoing and seemingly impossible to crack. Change can be better than a rest!

A certain genre can also hugely increase the M-Factor of your heroine and her story. *What Lies Beneath* could have been a sad drama about a woman coping with the empty-nest syndrome. When her only daughter goes to college she at least has the prospect of spending more time with her husband. Then she finds out not only has he had an affair, but he's murdered his young mistress. *What Lies Beneath* could also have been a taut woman-in-jeopardy thriller, but by making it supernatural, the story was elevated. *Julie and Julia* is a biopic about the French cookery chef Julia, but it's got a strong comedic tone, bringing to life the characters in a lively and engaging way. It is definitely nontraditional biopic fare!

GENRE AND YOUR STORY

First, ask yourself which genres you like writing and which you like watching. Are they the same? Then ask yourself why you avoid certain genres. You might be a brilliant dramatic writer, but drama could bore you. Then you might be put off that drama is often seen as the least commercial of genres and can be difficult to finance. If you talk yourself out of certain genres remember that the pendulum does always swing. A good screenplay takes a year to write (at least) then several more to make, unless you're working in TV, but the point is what's working for audiences today might be old news in several years time.

If you want your story to reach a target audience through online distribution, then the commercial arguments about what genres work might feel less relevant to you. If your audience is local, and you might have state subsidies, then you also might have more freedom. If you want a Hollywood studio to buy your film, it makes sense to find out what they are anticipating as future genres.

THE PRIMAL ARGUMENT

Some film theorists believe the appeal of certain genres is because they reflect patterns of survival that have evolved over thousands of years. They are compelling to the mainstream audience because we have primal drives about sex, birth, survival, and death, and we like to relate to these in a story. I think that if you're writing a heroine's story, primal is not all it seems.

In a traditionally masculine-orientated story with a hero, Getting the Girl is a stock phrase. We see it all the time. Actually, Getting the Good Girl is usually more to the point, after the male hero has literally or metaphorically killed off the seductive bad girl. He wants to protect and save the victim, the good girl. Victim saving is central to the traditional notion of heroic. The primal argument would say that men's stories symbolize the male need to create, protect, and defend the tribe. You need a good wife and mother of your children to help you do that, not an ego-centric seductress.

In a heroine's story, Getting the Guy is normally a result of the heroine realizing what she's doing wrong. She's making the wrong choices because of unresolved internal issues. Yes, this might lead her to Mr. Right. The primal argument would say, well, she needs Mr. Right to look after her and the children. But what about heroines who work? What about finding out after marriage that Mr. Right wasn't all he pretended? What if she divorces and takes a string of boyfriends? What if she is the seductress (remember Scarlett?). And worse, what if she is infertile? There's no primal reason for a woman to even exist after her children are grown up, so why do women live longer? Primal doesn't explain the rise of the bromance or bromedy in which men show love, affection, and loyalty to each other with lots of layers of union filling the story. It doesn't explain why genres evolve, and how these genres can even produce commercially successful films that show heroines and heroes doing it a different way. Primal seems to me to be a good excuse to give a biological explanation for the way things have been, but it's a little outdated for heroines' stories.

Let's take *Erin Brockovich*. It was a very successful film. No man saves single-mom Erin, and the only decent guy, George, is dumped by her when he grumbles about being taken for granted and stuck at home taking care of her kids. Let's call her family Tribe 1. Erin is not interested in creating a tribe with George, and vice versa. Her eventual boss at the legal firm, which we can call Tribe 2, gives her a chance after huge efforts on her side. Erin wants to heal and get compensation for a sick and violated community. Let's call it Tribe 3. Yes, death is threatening Tribe 3 in the form of water pollution and she, heroically, is saving them. But they are only under threat because corporate greed, in the form of Tribe 4, is more powerful. Anyway, the only reason in the first place why Erin is saving them is because her own family, Tribe 1, is under threat and because society, Tribe 5, has decreed Erin to be uneducated, unsuitable trailer trash with absolutely no status. As a poor, uneducated single mom, Tribe 5 isn't protecting her, it's starving her. The even further irony is that by taking on Tribes 2, 3, 4, and 5, Erin neglects Tribe 1, her primal tribe if there is one.

You can see what I'm getting at, can't you? Is *Erin Brockovich* a successful film on primal grounds because it reflects the basic need for survival in the form of hungry children and sick people, or was it successful because it made us think about the kind of lengths a single mom with no privileges has to go to, and why? The primal argument doesn't really explain stories that are more about *why*. More and more frequently, audiences turn to heroines' stories not for primal reasons but to think about why the world is so messed up. Don't we want to see heroines' showing that the world doesn't have to be like this?

The primal approach to screenwriting can often result in formulaic use of genre and stories that are designed primarily with commercial viability in mind. They don't challenge or question the status quo. So let's take a look at some of the more popular genres for heroines' stories, and why certain genres are better at helping your heroine be memorable.

GENRE BENDING: EVOLUTIONS IN GENRES

As the zeitgeist changes and affects women's lives, then so do genres and their conventions. Let's look at some of the most common genres for heroines and some of their most common conventions. Remember, genre conventions aren't carved in stone and frequently change as a genre evolves. The list of character conventions given under each genre are commonly found in film, but treat them as a way of triggering your imagination and breaking the mold, as much as sticking to the tried and tested.

- ∽ Drama
- ∽ Romance and "The Dramance"
- ∽ Romantic and "Dramantic" Comedy
- ∽ Comedy
- ∽ Thriller
- ∽ Supernatural Thriller
- ∽ Biopic
- ∽ Musical
- ∽ Science-Fiction

DRAMA

Drama can be an obvious choice if your story is about a woman coming to terms with her identity or dealing with very contemporary issues that affect her life. *Frozen River* and *Precious*, both recent films that were critically acclaimed and tough viewing, follow underprivileged heroines whose lives are blighted by extreme poverty. *Precious* is interesting because the narrative creatively weaves in musical and comedic elements to subvert the traditional drama genre, without diminishing the seriousness of its themes. These elements even serve to intensify the more harrowing story moments. But you wouldn't call the movie a comedy or even a dramedy. Legal drama series *The Good Wife* fuses the elements of the heroine's personal family crisis with the legal processes of clients seeking justice.

Subject matter for dramas is wide and diverse and often responds to contemporary social issues. I suspect we could see more dramas about poverty over the next decade, in which the individual cost of corporate risk and greed is exposed. Different cultures will deal with the economic crisis differently. Some cultures might produce dramas that dwell on the pain, but others might prefer to celebrate how an individual or group survive the difficult times and fight back.

Drama is the genre that has always produced lots of heroines' stories, but recently, they have been getting more Feel Good Femininity, reflecting women's needs for harmony and joy. If you can escape the script editor's sword cutting out all layers of union from your drama (due to an outdated belief that conflict and stakes must rule) then you might actually make your drama more compelling. Some dramas are just too tense or gloomy to watch. Remember that the layers of union are so much more than light relief, or they contrast to make the tension worse.

Heroine Character Conventions of Drama

- ∞ Heroines in dramas can be very isolated and Outsiders. If she's one of a group, the group can also be isolated somehow.

- ∞ The heroine can have a strong transformational arc, in which she changes for the better or worse. She might experience a new internal perspective on the world that she can't share with anyone else.

∾ One particular layer of conflict is dominant in her story: it could be Internal, Significant Other, Family, or Culture Conflict.

∾ Her personal transformation or change of circumstances is largely a result of her efforts in overcoming obstacles. If she relies on anyone, it's because she has sought out their help as part of her personal resurrection. *Maria Full of Grace* and *Precious* are examples this trend in self-reliance. However, *Frozen River* shows the reciprocity between women to help them deal with their problems.

∾ Your heroine feeling good is no bad thing!

ROMANCE AND THE DRAMANCE

The rise of the heroine-led romance has also led to changes in the way love is treated in stories. From epic romances, to quirky indie love stories, there has been a big shift from characters searching for love and finding it at the end of the story, to stories that follow what happens in love after the happy ending. Romance stories now question love so much that they can seem like dramas. In the same way, dramas can focus on the trials and tribulations of a love relationship. Let's take a look at character conventions of the traditional romance:

Heroine Character Conventions of the Romance

∾ The heroine wants to find love with another character who is given equal screen time. Both characters have either considerable internal or external obstacles to overcome to end up together.

∾ The heroine achieves a sad or happy ending in which she is either with her loved one or separated from him or her forever.

Old-style romance is feeling out of date. The emphasis on happily ever after could be a hangover of a masculine "hero's journey" orientation to the telling of love stories.

If a story is about a woman's experience of love after the happy ending, or her experiences of dealing with her own internal problems, which are getting in the way of love, calling it a drama feels outmoded and too generalized. Calling it a melodrama is even worse! It sounds like you've written it for Bette Davis or Joan Crawford, actresses from the 1940s. (On a personal note, I'd like to see the terms *melodrama* and *chick flick* both get slung out and fast). Heroines' experiences of love relationships after the happy ending are still about love and intimate relationship, after all.

It seems to me a new genre has evolved out of all these heroines' stories that deal with love and personal identity, both within and outside of relationships. I've come up with my own name for this new heroine-influenced genre — *the dramance*. It's a hybrid name that pays homage to both genres and symbolizes their union. You might not like it, and you might disagree. You might prefer to stick to melodrama but if we can have "bromance," I'm sticking with "dramance" — at least to get the point across that women's dramas frequently have a central intimate relationship at their heart, yet they aren't quite 'love stories.'

Let's think about an epic romance, *Cold Mountain*. On one level, the story conforms to the traditional romantic notion of lovers being kept apart by obstacles and conflicts, with a tragic ending robbing them of a life together. But most of Ida's story is really about her own evolution as a woman. Ida meets Inman, lets him kiss her, and before you know it, he's been conscripted. She had time to realize she fancies him but not to get to know him. All she has is his pledge that he will come back, leaving her with a fantasy and a promise. These are really important to her sense of hope, but what she really needs is someone there for her, to provide support and help her after she loses her father, money, and servants. This comes in the form of redneck Ruby, who enters Ida's life, and the two women develop a strong relationship. Through Ruby, Ida gains a friend and generally develops as a person. Her story is full of idealized, loving feelings for Inman, and a growing real love of Ruby, but it is only Inman who follows the solitary hero's path back to Ida.

Something similar happens with *The Hours*. The three heroines all have very important intimate relationships with men, and all these relationships are the source of huge internal conflict in the women. Virginia Woolf kills herself partly because she cannot bear to put Leonard, her husband, through another of her bouts of madness. Laura, the depressed housewife in 1950s L.A., cannot endure her life with her husband, although guilt has kept her in the marriage. Clarissa, in 1990s

Manhattan, is emotionally bound up with her dying friend. By caring for him, she feels less empty inside.

In both these movies, only the heroines' experiences are followed, but their intimate relationships are the most powerful source of conflict. This is beyond drama, because loving relationships are central. I think they are dramances! Another big feature of the dramance is the importance of the layers of union in the story. *Iris* and *Away from Her*, both stories about dementia, use layers of union, sometimes in flashback, to celebrate the women's capacity for life and love before their terrible plight. Although both aren't strictly heroine's stories because the men characters' POV is dominant, the women characters' processes of losing their minds are sensitively chronicled. *The Notebook*, another narrative that explores female dementia, has a romance storyline set in the past and a dramance storyline set in the present.

Heroine Character Conventions of the Dramance

∽ The heroine's sense of identity is deeply affected by her relationship. She needs to resolve her problems for the sake of her identity and/or the relationship.

∽ If she doesn't have an intimate relationship, she needs to work on her issues to be able to love.

∽ She might resolve these issues by the end of her story, but whether she commits to a relationship or not isn't an important feature of the story's ending. If she is in a relationship, the question whether her relationship will end or resolves itself is open as well. In a nutshell, endings can be open.

ROMANTIC AND DRAMANTIC COMEDY

The same fusion between romantic comedies and "dramantic" comedies can also be seen when a heroine leads the story. Romantic comedies with heroines explore all the conflicts that get in the way of the heroine and her potential lover being together. In romantic comedies, the heroine spends most of her time enduring conflict-ridden dynamics with her potential loved one who also occupies a great deal of, if not equal amounts, of screen time. At the end of the narrative, as surely as night turns to day, the heroine gets her happy ending with her ideal man. Examples include the dating game (*Bridget Jones's Diary*), weddings (*The Wedding Planner*, *27 Dresses*), one-night stands (*What Happens in Vegas*), and marriages of convenience (*The Proposal*).

Heroine Character Conventions in Romantic Comedy

- The character has major baggage getting in the way of loving a man (or woman) that is clearly her soul mate. The heroine cannot recognize this until she's dealt with her baggage by spending as much time as possible fighting with, and resisting, the potential lover! He might even share the same levels of resistance to her. Think of *When Sally Met Harry*.

- The heroine is driven by unresolved Internal Conflict. However, Significant Other Conflict is a dominant layer in the story.

- The heroine is blind to her faults or baggage, particularly as her potential lover points them out. She only begins to recognize them as her feelings toward him change, and she is motivated to change his perception.

- By the end of her story, the heroine achieves both Internal and Significant Other Union.

- The heroine attending a wedding, her own or someone else's, is a frequent event at the end of the story. Some kind of symbolic union usually takes place, even if it is a verbal promise of a future together.

The dramantic comedy has some important differences to the romantic comedy. The most obvious is that the heroine's story does not resolve her need to get together with her loved one. The heroine's story takes priority, as we watch her sort out her own problems. It's rare to have the potential loved one have any of his or her own scenes without the heroine also there. In a nutshell, the dramance and the dramantic comedy tell her story, even if love is part of it.

Julie and Julia is a great example of a dramatic comedy. Both heroines have hugely important relationships with their partners, and the women's quests wouldn't even exist without the men in their lives. *The Holiday*, *The Break-up*, *He's Just Not That Into You*, and *Sex and the City: The Movie* are also dramatic comedies. Carrie and Big have found love at the beginning but lose it with a monumental Test of Trust. The rest of the narrative follows Carrie dealing with her wounds and making changes to her life. She needs to grow as a person, on her own and with the support of her female friends, in order to function in a couple (which, by the end of the narrative, she can). This is no romantic comedy, neither is it a straight comedy. It's a dramatic comedy!

Heroine Character Conventions in Dramatic Comedy

∽ The heroine has an intimate relationship that sustains her or sabotages her sense of self. If she's getting to know a man, she's got major work to do on her emotional baggage.

∽ Internal Conflict is a dominant layer of conflict.

∽ The heroine's love interest doesn't have his or her own story line. He or she isn't in scenes without the heroine, except rarely.

∽ If the heroine has an intimate relationship, the partner has a powerful impact on her self-esteem, good or bad. In *Julie and Julia* the male partners of Julie and Julia are supportive and loving, helping to build their partners up and getting involved with the quests. In *The Holiday*, the heroines' dodgy relationships at least propel them to work on their emotional baggage.

∽ Bad relationships are jettisoned by the heroine as her emotional wounds are resolved.

∽ The heroine's story doesn't necessarily end with a union of the lovers or definite closure. Endings can feel quite open.

∽ Internal Union, a sense of fulfilment, is a powerful layer of union at the end of her story.

COMEDY

As relationships are so central to so many heroines' stories, what about the straight-up female-led comedy? Are there any that don't focus on the heroine's relationship, either because she needs one and gets one (romantic comedy) or has one or wants one while she gets on with other things (dramantic comedy). Sometimes the writer's need to add a relationship is not the right decision, because what would make a perfectly good comedy in its own right tries at the same time to be a romantic comedy. *Baby Mama* and *Confessions of a Shopaholic* were both weaker because they had to cram a potential relationship on top of the heroine solving her major problem. Neither film felt like it knew what it really wanted to be, a romantic comedy or a comedy. They didn't work as dramantic comedies either, because the relationships with men weren't central enough, and they stuck too closely to the romantic comedy pattern of union only at the end. There are more pure comedies with older heroines (*Calendar Girls* and *Tea with Mussolini*) or school girls (*St. Trinian's*). TV shows like *Weeds* and *Ugly Betty* are good examples where the comedy stays comedy.

There's definitely a gap in the market for comedy movies with heroines. We need more *Calendar Girls*, for instance. What is the female equivalent of the bromance — a feminine dramance version of *Thelma and Louise* without the cliff plunge? Why are we so reluctant to make comedies for heroines that are just funny situations? Maybe we don't always need a man.

Heroine Character Conventions in Comedy

- ∞ The heroine's relationships, if she has any, are minor in comparison to her main problem.

- ∞ A group of heroines might lead the story.

- ∞ Comedy is derived from the heroine's blind spot, which generates a lot of internal and external complications.

- ∞ The heroine's main problem gets solved at the end of the story, but not necessarily in the way the heroine expected it.

∞ Because she's not relationship orientated, she might be on a quest or accidentally find herself in a predicament she has to get out of, and fast.

THRILLER

Just like comedies, we need more solid thrillers with heroines. It's rare for a heroine to have the solitary and dark persona that male heroes can have, instead, an overwhelming desire for vengeance is more common in the thriller heroine. Watch the South Korean *Lady Vengeance* for a heroine consumed with the need for retaliation. Very frequently, a thriller with a heroine will have secondary story of a relationship or quasi-love relationship. This is normally with a man, and there is a good chance he will have an active role in helping her at the end. We see this very often. Even in *The Brave One*, the heroine needs to be saved from herself by an understanding man. It is rare for the heroine to be saved by another woman.

This is the opposite of the male hero in a thriller. If he has a secondary love or relationship story going on, he will either save her, or be unable to help her (*Chinatown*).

Heroine Character Conventions in a Thriller

∞ The heroine can be a woman in jeopardy with a vulnerable child to protect.

∞ Betrayal by a loved one can put her in jeopardy. Revenge or some kind of equalizing motivation often drives the heroine.

∞ She has a complex and life-threatening mystery to solve.

∞ The heroine often has some personal Internal Wound that is re-flected by the external crime/problem/mystery (i.e., a very clear Metaphoric Wound).

∞ The heroine might be motivated to save a more helpless woman or group of women or vulnerable people.

∞ If she is saving a man she loves, he has put himself in jeopardy because he was helping her first.

SUPERNATURAL THRILLER

Heroines are often found in supernatural thrillers. They can be ghosts or summoned by ghosts. *Gothika* and *What Lies Beneath* both have female ghosts that seek the heroine out in order to protect her from her husband and expose his disloyalty and his crime. It is a metaphor for the abandoned mistress who was not able to break up the family unit because the man rejected her for his wife and continues to live a lie. More memorable is the matricidal heroine in *The Others*. Grace is a restless ghost, haunted by her own guilt for killing her children. TV shows include *Medium* and *Ghost Whisperer*, in which the heroine solves a case by using her supernatural powers.

Twilight is a supernatural romantic thriller. The vampire Edward is Bella's soul mate. His love "possesses" her. Her quest is to be with him forever, but the antagonistic forces working against their union are numerous.

Heroine Character Conventions in a Supernatural Thriller

- ∞ The heroine can be "summoned" as a supernatural force enters her life. Alternatively, she is the force. The force symbolizes a blind spot or a wound that must be healed in the heroine, like an alter ego who represents a victim role choice the heroine may have unwittingly made. For example, marrying a man who will prove to be really bad.

- ∞ Betrayal is a powerful form of Significant Other Conflict in the story. If it doesn't affect the heroine directly, it affects the ghosts whose problems she deals with.

- ∞ Guilt is a powerful form of Internal Conflict.

- ∞ The heroine's sanity is often doubted. Even she begins to doubt her own internal logic and judgment.

- ∞ The supernatural force triggers a quest of truth and survival for the heroine, usually instigated by a horrible event.

- ∞ Deception of the heroine by her loved one is a frequent revelation as a result of the quest.

∞ The heroine survives the ordeal with the help of the supernatural power but only after her quest has led to the truth.

∞ If she is supernatural or summoned, the heroine might live her life in one perpetual cycle with no resolution. The story doesn't have closure and instead feels circular. If she is the lead in a TV series, she repeatedly attempts to solve supernatural dilemmas throughout the episodes.

BIOPIC

The biopic isn't strictly a genre, as it doesn't have recognizable conventions. It's simply a way of categorizing films with real-life characters. A biopic story can actually be in any genre you like, but it is far more common that writers choose dramas, sometimes dramantic comedies (*Julie and Julia*), dramances (*The Hours*), and sometimes even thrillers (*Elizabeth*). By being imaginative with your choice of genre, you can really make your biopic screenplay stand out. Biopics can have fictional elements, such as contemporary characters whose lives are somehow changed by coming into contact with the historical character.

If a heroine is dark and complex, nine times out of ten she will be a real-life character (or if fictional, from Japanese, South Korean, or French cinema). In the United States and United Kingdom, a compulsive or deeply dangerous heroine is more likely to make it to the screen if she is a real life person, which says a lot about cultural differences. This makes biopics good to study for character complexity. Examples of biopics with dark heroines are *Monster*, *Mrs. Parker and the Vicious Circle*, and *La Vie en Rose*.

Heroine Character Conventions for Biopics

These conventions are broad because ultimately character conventions will reflect those of the genre you choose to write the biopic in:

∞ The heroine is a real-life character.

∞ The heroine is known or unknown but will have some claim to fame.

∞ If she is not known widely, the story will aim to highlight her achievement or the reason she should be known.

Once you have chosen your true-life character, your biggest challenge will be using true-life facts to shape a dramatic story. You might wish to use the principles, exercises, and questionnaires in this book in order to help you build your heroine's character and select story information from her real life to make her memorable.

MUSICAL

The rise in popularity of musicals such as *Eight Women*, *Chicago*, *Moulin Rouge*, *Mamma Mia!*, and *Nine* has put this genre firmly on the entertainment map for heroines' stories. Music, singing, and dancing bring a deeply joyous important element to these films. They bring a whole new layer of harmony to the viewing experience, and judging by their success, this is what audiences want. Unless lyrics are your strong point, team up with a good song writer to write a good musical!

Heroine Character Convention in a Musical

∞ Two-dimensional characterization and stereotypes aren't such a scourge to the writer of the musical.

∞ Heroines find love, are competitive with others, pitch themselves against a dominant patriarch figure who seeks to control them, and have mother/daughter relationships.

∞ The most important thing is that heroines express their emotional journeys and experiences by singing and dancing through most of them!

∞ The heroine or heroines tend to end up victorious or fulfilled.

SCIENCE FICTION

Sci-fi stories allow great scope for the development of hugely diverse female characters from worlds with very different values, traditions, and roles. This kind of imaginative freedom might really appeal to you if you are jaded with life on planet Earth.

Gender difference is frequently a nonissue in the sci-fi film unless it is concerned with the reproduction of the human race, when women characters and the right to their bodies tend to be under threat, such *The Handmaid's Tale*, which gave a nightmarish vision of scientific interference with reproduction. Or they work for the bad guys as scientists who are responsible for new evolutions in the human form. *Terminator Salvation* and *Avatar* both have women characters in powerful scientific roles.

Heroine Character Conventions in Science Fiction

The heroine's femininity isn't an issue, unless there are reproductive elements to the story. The heroine's skills and brains count more. She has to be capable of functioning in outer space, using high-tech equipment, dealing with aliens, and being a brilliant scientist.

UNPOPULAR GENRES FOR HEROINES

By this I mean those main genres in which heroines don't tend to be featured very often or they are featured in very stereotypical ways. These are:

∾ Horror

∾ Action-adventure and Action Thrillers

In horror films, female characters are traditionally either heroines (young, blonde, and attractive), victims (unlikeable traits), or female forces of evil (possessed or born evil). Masculine-orientated stereotypes (good-girl victims and seductresses) can rule the day, making the horror a difficult genre to crack if your heroine is too complex. In horror, morality in characterization has no shades of grey. In the past, this has been because a large percentage of your audience is likely to be male and/or under thirty. Layers of union are virtually nonexistent in horror films, as they are designed to create extremely tense and suspenseful viewing experiences.

The Descent pushed the boundaries of horror by having a group of female friends enter a cave filled with cannibalistic hybrid humans. The dynamics between the female friends are reflected in themes of love, female bonding, and motherhood against a backdrop of survival. Sarah, the heroine, is an incomplete heroine mourning the loss of her child and husband, only to end up having to fight for her own survival as her friends are killed off one by one. Whether further evolutions of female characterization in the horror genre will widen the audience is a big question.

Heroines in action-adventure and action thrillers have also been evolving. Although they are frequently still young and beautiful, their characterization is getting more complex. They usually have their own agendas, backstory wounds, and desire to fulfill their own missions. *Mr. and Mrs. Smith*, *Quantum of Solace*, and *The Incredibles* all have women characters who defy the stereotypical female of the action-adventure by being more complex. It would be nice to see an older action-adventure heroine, as unlikely as that may seem.

Wrapping Up...

Genres continuously evolve, and there are numerous subgenres always emerging. Different cultures also have very different genres, and it can open your eyes to watch a great deal of recent films from other countries to see their conventions.

EXERCISE: GENRE CONVENTIONS

Go to the theater or rent out three or four movies in a certain genre that you normally avoid. It doesn't matter if they have heroes or heroines, but try to get a selection with both. Try to identify all the conventions in the genre that make it recognizable. Look at the character conventions, using my approach above.

Even if you have worked out the genre for your story, think about how you could change it to the genre you have been studying. Does it make it more interesting? The purpose of this exercise isn't to make you necessarily change your genre, but it's good to get out of habits. It could even encourage you to think about another genre.

UNSUNG HEROINES

Chapter 9

By now I hope you are well on the way to knowing who your heroine is, the story she's leading, and all the factors that will make her compelling, unique, and completely unforgettable. If you haven't got a project on the go, maybe your imagination will have been fired by some of these ideas.

There are still some grossly underrepresented women in film and TV, such as lesbians, disabled women, women of different ethnic groups, and older women. As Whoopi Goldberg once joked, Tiana, the animated African American princess in *The Princess and the Frog* is black, but she spends 70% of the film as a frog so that's okay.

Then there's the lack of certain kinds of heroines leading certain kind of genres, such as thriller and action-adventure. It is all too easy to narrow the scope of your story ideas and concepts when you have a heroine in mind. It's as if we still want to give our heroes and heroines very different territory to roam in the worlds of our stories. We are still risk averse in what we allow heroines to do and be. If a female character takes wild risks and chooses career over love and family, then in movies she's still more likely to be the heroine of a biopic, a fantasy, or sci-fi (*Monsters vs Aliens*). On TV, she's still likely to be in a procedural or investigative series.

Let's take a film with a hero, written and produced by a male team, *The Departed*. It was hailed for its brilliant characterization and complex morality. Now do the mental exercise of swapping Jack Nicolson's character Frank with a woman. Let's call her Francesca, and imagine Meryl Streep or Judi Dench playing her as the nasty gang leader who rules by extortion and torture but has a soft spot for her surrogate daughter. Imagine Leonardo di Caprio's character played by Cameron Diaz. She has no kids, no family, and a high IQ, and life has shaped her into being a good chameleon. Written well, with Scorsese directing, without resorting to stereotypes that either sexualize or demonize the women, this mythical female-led rendition of *The Departed* could be a compelling film, exploring the rarely shown scenes of female power, violence, and paranoia. Oh yes, you'd have to make the shrink (who to my mind was the weakest character in the film) a passive and easily manipulated young man who looks good with his clothes off. This film wouldn't be untrue or unlikely. There are plenty of ruthless and manipulative women in the real world who wouldn't think twice about killing. You might be ahead of your time if you wrote it. I bet audiences would love it.

FORGETTABLE HEROINES

Remember the M-Factor? Lots of heroines simply don't have it. Their stories might, but nine times out of ten they have suffered the greatest threat known to female characterization: Heroine Softening.

The requirement of making female characters softer was explored in-depth by Lizzie Francke in *Script Girls* (1994), in which she interviewed many women screenwriters and directors in Hollywood about their work. Many of her interviewees were pressured by producers and executives to tone down strength and complexity in their female characters. She highlighted the conservatism women felt affected their projects and the fear some producers have for female characters that are too dark or complex. Heroine Softening is a syndrome that you should be aware of because it can still happen.

HEROINE SOFTENING

In the best-case scenario, your heroine will be close to your vision as the writer, the happy outcome of a rewarding creative journey with others you may be working with. If you feel under pressure to make her softer, warmer, or nicer, you can use her M-Factor like an ace up your sleeve. It also might help you to know some of the reasons why complex traits can still be less acceptable for women.

The roots of this double standard, I believe, are to be found in our earliest life experiences and the fact that women do most of the mothering. You may not agree with the explanation I'm going to give, but you might see some grain of truth in it. The mother, in a child's psyche, is the soft and gentle caregiver, as well as the all-powerful being we depend on. As we grow up, culture reinforces attitudes and expectations of what women are supposed to be, reflecting or even contradicting our unconscious feelings about our earliest role models, both male and female. A fear of female domination and anger, and a craving for gentleness and kindness in women can equate to deeply uncomfortable feelings about the scary or unsympathetic female. She should be soft and loving! This discomfort, or "dread" as some theorists have called it, results in the fantasy females of men's stories and the deeply conflicted heroines of women's stories. Very simplistically, the Hero seeks a vulnerable female (the opposite of their mothers) who needs saving, and for whom the man can prove himself as worthy. And the Heroine? She experiences an identity crisis! She wants to be saved and completed by her soul mate Hero (e.g., *Cinderella*, *Sleeping Beauty*, *Snow White*, *Elizabeth Bennett*, and *Bridget Jones*), at the same time, she only has her mother as her deepest role model. In the close relationship or when the heroine becomes a mother, family patterns re-emerge. The Heroine feels let down or empty, and the Hero's getting restless. He didn't sign up for a gorgon or a needy child. He thought he'd found the maiden! As for her, she's thinking where has my Prince Charming gone?

This is a generalization, of course. As the gender gap closes, and culture gives men and women more freedom to live how we want, our stories, and what we like to think of as unchanging mythic patterns, can and actually do change! Increasingly, heroines' stories deal not with the "happy ever after" but with "what happens next?" And heroes? Maybe now they are finding the soft maiden and overburdened mother within themselves.

The ongoing existence of stereotypes is evidence of centuries-long strictly defined masculine and feminine roles. The flipside of soft heroines is the range of negative stereotypes of women — the nag, hag, evil stepmother, ugly sister, evil witch, vulturistic seductress — and their film and TV manifestations — femme fatale, bunny boiler, MILF, black widow, raving nympho, axe-wielding lesbian, welfare queen, difficult diva, and blonde bimbo. Negative stereotypes reveal misogyny about women. On the whole they don't resonate truthfully with women, but we still take them to heart. But the trouble with the ongoing existence of any stereotype is that it sets up parameters in your mind, like a keep-out fence. If your heroine is too wounded or complex, she might share some traits that we are used to seeing in a stereotypical character. She's entered the forbidden zone of our unconscious, and we fear everyone will hate her.

THE DEVELOPMENT PROCESS

Producers and development executives, both male and female, might project their own experiences of women as well as their feelings about what women should be like onto the female character. They might genuinely believe the best chance of commercial success is to have a strongly likeable and sympathetic heroine. You might find concerns can be raised about:

- ∞ A heroine's selfishness.

- ∞ A heroine's emotional wounds affecting her ability to be warm and open.

- ∞ A heroine being too sexually aggressive or too radical in her expressions of desire.

- ∞ A heroine's age or attractiveness.

- ∞ A heroine's lack of conventional femininity.

There's no easy answer to these expectations. You have to manage the process and trust your convictions.

How to Handle Heroine Softening

If people you work with, co-writers, producers, or directors have ideas about the heroine that veer wildly from your vision, then the two Cs — *clarity* and *compromise* — now have to become your modus operandi.

Clarity

You need to define exactly what isn't working. Prepare to be politely challenging. If comments are vague, it's your job to tease out exactly what isn't working and why. If you don't, you risk seriously misfiring with the next draft.

A writer told me that a producer said to her "I don't fancy her" about the heroine, as if that was an important criteria of characterization! It certainly might improve the potential movie's prospects for satisfying the male audience! If something similar happens to you, you have the interesting task as writer to find out what kind of women he does fancy and what puts him off. If his vision of women is for softness and vulnerability, then you will have to use the M-Factor argument. Cite all those heroines who stand out because they weren't soft and vulnerable, or because they dealt with rarely seen situations for women. The ones that did big box office are usually the most sensible to cite — Scarlett O' Hara, Juno, Dora in *Central Station*, *Thelma and Louise*, Ripley, Donna in *Mamma Mia!*, Margaret in *The Proposal*, or Lisbeth in *The Girl with the Dragon Tattoo*. Or choose heroines that you personally like and why.

Remind your team that if she is too soft your heroine (and the film) could risk being unforgettable. Suggest that the only hope for the film being memorable would be to give the soft and uncomplicated heroine a very dramatic story. From *Precious* to Fiona in *Shrek*, heroines can be truly likeable, kind, and loving, but to be memorable they have to have a dire problem!

Take *Changeling*. A perfect mother, saintly and beautiful, suffers the most unimaginable series of horrors: Her son disappears from home while she is at work, and then the police insist another boy is her missing child. Christine Collins' outrage and desperate denial leads to the police incarcerating her in a psychiatric asylum. This leads to the second half of the story being led by male heroes, a priest and a detective who ultimately save the heroine from injustice. This is the trouble with true stories. If your true life character had no real power or autonomy over her life, at least by sticking with her POV gives her a chance of memorability rather than the story or another character leading the action.

Changeling is a good example of heavy viewing. The layers of conflict are very dominant, and internal conflict is limited. There are a few layers of union, except some female bonding in the institution and compassion from other characters for the heroine. The role choice of Victim is dominant, until Christine reflects the Amazon role choice when she defends the other female patients. What could be worse than losing your son after you had not been very pleasant that morning? What if she'd snapped at him? The heroine is not memorable, but her harrowing situation is. It is a horrible event, and a story worth telling, but the main character suffers from a loss of complexity by being the perfect mom.

Compromise

If you can't compromise, screenwriting might be an unsatisfying profession for you. Your role as writer is to play your vital role in creating a screenplay that you, the director, and the producers consider to be good enough to find a wide audience. It's about taking notes, listening to feedback, and remaining open. Nine times out of ten, if many people raise the same concerns about your story, they might just have a point.

The art of compromise involves a genuine willingness to listen, but too much compromise can kill genuine art. Your voice, choices, and judgments as the screenwriter are essential components to the finished art form. You aren't just providing a blueprint, no matter who calls the script that! A theme is not something that comes to life on set; it is born on the page. Remember, some people you work with might not even share your understanding of what a theme is, but they will feel the power of your story if you have managed to retain your creative vision. Screenwriting is a particularly challenging form of creative writing. It's an art, a craft, and a science. If you feel strongly enough about any character, principle, or dramatic element, stick to your guns.

MANAGING YOUR CAREER

Although this book is really about your heroine, I just wanted to share with you some final thoughts about developing your career in order to help you become a memorable writer.

For the Nurturers Out There

If you are a Nurturer of others, finding physical and mental space is a priority for your creative and career success. Some lucky people have the amazing ability to just switch off whatever domestic hurly-burly is going on around them and find the right mental focus. They don't let the needs and demands of other get to them.

Women often find it harder to switch off their need to look after others. Sometimes they don't even want to give up or share this role. Whether this is a biological brain-wiring problem, the effect of estrogen, or is a product of being brought up to care for others, the result can be the same. Nurturing others can limit your output.

As men have sought to become more equal and active partners on the parenting front, and as more women have shared the role, they too feel that finding time for creativity is an issue. I talk to a great deal of parents in my seminars about this, and I am a writer mom and step-mom, so I know what a constant dilemma finding a balance is.

Life might feed inspiration but at some point the inspiration has to be translated into a developed project. Life can also kill inspiration if it's too frenetic or demanding. Exhaustion doesn't help art, neither does a fragmented mind. You need to find isolation, and your project needs incubation. What you focus on grows, simple as that.

Working in blocks of time might help you. One writer I know does what she can around her busy schedule, but in the early stages she never feels submerged enough. Then periodically she goes away for a week for complete isolation. During this time she can pull everything together. The themes, stories, and characters start to click. The art takes form. She goes back to busy life feeling much more in control and with a real sense of progress. As her project develops and gains strength, she finds it easier to feel in control even when she's working from home and doing her day job. There are other ways to get the necessary isolation if you don't like the idea of going away. The novelist Fay Weldon burnt the "early morning oil" to get a great deal of writing done before her children woke up. Remember — your memorable heroine is worth it!

FUTURE HEROINES

As we finish, let's anticipate the future and the kinds of stories heroines will be leading. Wouldn't it be great if your next heroine is one of those truly unforgettable female characters who are remembered for decades? Clever writers can dream up characters that somehow represent exactly what the audience almost needs to see and hear, sum up the zeitgeist, and ring true, even in a sci-fi film. So ask yourself:

⊛ What kind of films would you like to see with a woman in the lead?

⊛ What have you never seen a heroine do or be?

⊛ What stories are yet to be told?

⊛ What changes do you anticipate in women's lives over the next decade?

As women's lives have been and remain in flux, it makes sense to look at all the changes, wherever you are in the world. Women's lives always go forward, as the evolutions in movies and TV shows reflect. Take the vampire movies *Twilight*, *New Moon*, and *Eclipse*. Their prime audience is young and female. The characterization of the heroine Bella, and the focus of her story on unconditional and eternal love, obviously communicates something very powerful to the teenage girls who are fans of these movies. Bella has a dark and all-conquering passion for her vampire lover Edward; she is heroically protective of him and will go as far as sacrificing her mortality for him. Bella and Edward's love represents the ultimate union of soul mates. Teenage girls' capacity to idolize and obsess about men reflects a yearning for intimacy and togetherness that boys of the same age tend not to experience as strongly. But Bella's characterization also reflects strength, autonomy, and empowerment — qualities that teenage girls want to relate to. She's no passive heroine waiting to be saved. Bella is deep and not conventionally "girlie." She hates shopping and fashion, mumbles when she speaks, and even bonds with guys more easily than she does with girls. She's memorable because she's an individual who resonates truthfully.

Something's Gotta Give, It's Complicated, Calendar Girls, Damages, Mamma Mia!, and *Ladies in Lavender* reflect different aspects about women getting older and their feelings about their bodies, sexuality, and relationships. Although Feel Good Femininity, these stories are a long way from the acceptable clichés of *The Golden Girls* and *Miss Marple*. The older female audience is only getting bigger, and women everywhere may well want to be fulfilled and entertained by stories that respect they have sex drives, are menopausal, are still attractive to the right men, *and* want to be a grandmother. They also might want to see more Jane Tennisons and older Ripleys who take on complex quests and missions — women who are clever strategists, brilliant thinkers, champions of causes, intrepid explorers, and risk-taking decision makers. I predict a rise in stories with older heroines or else the thirty-five-plus female audience will remain untapped.

And back on the family front? What about the growing number of forty-something moms who will have teenagers in their sixties, those women who chose never have had children (and for whom this isn't a soul-destroying tragedy), and the rise of stepmoms? Who will tell these women's stories? Maybe it will be you!

Then there's your own culture, wherever in the world you are. What kinds of success stories for heroines have emerged? What are the conditions like for women screenwriters in your industries? It's interesting to watch movies from different cultures. You can get a good idea of what I call "zeitgeist" issues going on for women in a particular country. Take French cinema as an example. *Villa Amalia, The Piano Teacher, Leaving*, and *I've Loved You So Long* show painfully honest experiences of love and loss. The French have made an iconic art form out of internal conflict in women and are not afraid of giving audiences heroines who question their lives and make exceptionally difficult choices. For a nation that gave their female citizens the vote decades after the U.S. and the U.K., their storytelling has definitely made up for lost time! French heroines seem to be angry and are not afraid to show it.

As climate change threatens our very existence, terrorism remains a constant threat, and the global economy battles its worst-ever depression, maybe we all want more escapism in the form of fantasy, fun, and feel good movies. Or maybe the pendulum will swing to a preference for films and TV series that inform and reflect our questioning values. But there's a good chance the female audience in particular will continue to want heroines' stories that reflect the continued flux in their lives *and* push boundaries in the storytelling. If the male audience is discovering a need for more emotionally expressive stories, as the rise of the bromance and bromedy testify, then there's a good chance an opposite shift can happen for the female audience with films like a female version of *The Departed*, in which typical feminine roles take backseat. As heroes become more relationship orientated, will heroines of all ages take on more action? Will the gender gap close in our stories, so that heroes and heroines can be truly interchangeable in leading strong stories? Maybe unhelpful expectations and outmoded sex roles will finally disappear altogether, and we will all focus on our communal strengths in protecting the planet and living in peace.

I sincerely wish your memorable heroine is someone who shows the way.

EXERCISE: SCREENWRITER'S STORY QUESTIONNAIRE

Imagine you are in charge of a committee for the protection of memorable heroines. Ask yourself:

∾ How are you going to make sure people understand what your heroine stands for? Write your very own Memorable Heroine's Manifesto!

∾ How do you find time for yourself and your writing? What could you do differently to increase your satisfaction with your work, and your output?

Finally, complete the Screenwriter's Story Questionnaire, the last in this book.

Good luck!

SCREENWRITER'S STORY QUESTIONNAIRE

1. What is your heroine's name?

2. What is her M–Factor?

3. What is her dominant story type?

4. What is the theme of your story?

5. What is the Metaphoric Wound?

6. What role choices does your heroine particularly identify with and how?

7. What Phases resonate with your story structure?

8. What are the greatest sources of conflict for your heroine?

9. What are the greatest sources of union for your heroine?

10. What genre have you chosen?

11. Who is the perfect actress to play your heroine?

12. What is the title of your story?

A HEROINE IN ACTION: AN ANALYSIS OF *JUNO*

Chapter 10

Juno was written by Diablo Cody who went on to win the Oscar for best original screenplay. As a sixteen-year-old who goes on a quest to find the right adoptive parents for her unborn child, Juno immediately resonated with all types of audiences all over the world. Why did she hold such appeal? What was the secret to Juno that made this low-budget movie with a relatively unknown cast such a big hit?

By relating the principles of *The Woman in the Story* to Juno's story, we can see how they could be used to create a truly memorable heroine like Juno.

JUNO'S SUPERTHEME

Juno is definitely not a Familiar Femininity film. There is nothing conservative about the story, which subverts a great deal of prejudice about pregnant sixteen-year-olds. But it hasn't got a Fighting Femininity Supertheme either, because Juno isn't fighting the system. She doesn't feel that life is unfair. Like many teenage girls, Juno was born long after feminism, and she's not unduly concerned with "equality." Her dad and stepmom Bren raise her, and her real mother lives far away with a new batch of kids. Juno has no meaningful contact with her, except sending her the annual gift of a cactus. Neither has *Juno* got a Feel Good Femininity Supertheme because *Juno* is not about celebrating Juno's femininity as a young, pregnant teenager.

Juno doesn't deal with her abortion dilemma with a feminist perspective. She does simply what many teenagers do, gets carried away by her sexual urges and has unprotected sex with Paulie Bleeker. Now she's paying the price of that risk; she takes full responsibility for her situation, even pushing Paulie away because her identity is in turmoil. She takes it for granted she can get an abortion, and she makes up her own mind that it just doesn't feel right. The male characters love and nurture her. If Juno has a problem with either gender, it is probably with women, but she doesn't think consciously in these terms. That's up to the audience to work out.

Juno is a Future Femininity Film. Juno happens to be female, happens to get pregnant, and takes herself on a quest to do something about it.

JUNO'S M-FACTOR

Juno's most compulsive need is defensiveness. This means she pushes people away to protect herself. Being emotionally open is not her style. It could leave her open to rejection. Juno's most irreverent trait is defiance. She won't be told what to do, even when it's in her best interests. She will do what she wants, when she wants. Finally, Juno's most charismatic trait is her verbal dexterity of wit. Now, do the simple equation! Juno's M-Factor is naïve tough-talker. Juno thinks she knows it all, spouts defensive back-chat, and learns the hard way that she might have got things wrong.

ROLE CHOICES

Juno identifies, consciously or unconsciously, mainly with the role choices of heroine, lover, mother, and dependant. What kind of heroine is Juno? At first she's a Questing Heroine, on a mission to lose her virginity with Paulie Bleeker. As soon as she finds out she is pregnant, she becomes both an Incomplete Heroine, having cut herself off from Paulie, and a Questing Heroine, in her effort to find the right adoptive parents for her unborn child. At school and elsewhere, she's an Outsider, being pregnant so young.

The mother role choice is at the heart of Juno, as all the female characters identify with this role choice in different ways. Juno is a pregnant teenager, a soon-to-be mom. She consciously wants to be a good mother, not by keeping the baby, because she knows instinctively she's neither old enough nor desirous to give up her youth. The best she can do for her baby is find the right parents. Vanessa aspires to be the perfect, idealized mother but can't get pregnant. Juno consciously decides that together, Mark and Vanessa are the perfect parents. She is ambivalent toward the control-freak side of Vanessa, initially preferring Mark, who is more fun and easy going. As a child, and still a dependant who has little responsibility, Mark is more available to her. However, Vanessa's desire for motherhood is so strong that Juno comes to realize that Vanessa will be a brilliant mother for her child on an emotional level. It is not just for surface reasons, such as affluence and a perfect home.

When it comes to Paulie Bleeker, Juno identifies mainly with the Believer role choice, as a Lover and Rival. Her feelings for Paulie lead to her pregnancy and then make her reject him. Projecting her rejection as him dumping her, she becomes the Rival to a female classmate.

STORY TYPE, THEME, AND METAPHORIC WOUND OF *JUNO*

Juno's Story Type

Rites of Passage is the dominant story type because so many things in her story are a first for Juno. She's found her first love, lost her virginity, is pregnant for the first time, and giving her child up to adoption. These are all major life events. These Rites of Passages will not propel Juno into adulthood, but they will enable her to learn more responsibility, to herself and others.

The Theme of Juno

"Your true family are the people who are there for you." Juno's underlying message is that no matter whether they are blood relatives or not, the people who form your true family are those who don't let you down and who let you in. Juno is not let down by her father Mac and her stepmom Bren. They are there for her on every level. Vanessa does not let Juno down and proves herself, unlike Mark, to be the true parent of Juno's unborn baby. As a lover, Paulie Bleeker never lets Juno down either. Brenda is Juno's true mother and helps her practically and emotionally through the pregnancy. Like a true mother, she tolerates Juno's adolescent testing of her and knows her weaknesses.

Juno's *Metaphoric Wound Is Parental Loss*

Remember, you use the Wounds and Gifts Principles to discover a Metaphoric Wound. Juno's Internal Wound is the abandonment by her own mother. This hurts Juno, and she is very upfront about it, rubbishing the cacti her mother sends her (that she hasn't thrown away, significantly).

Juno's Internal Gift is her verbal dexterity as a form of defensiveness. This is how she has learnt to cope with pain. Although jokes and banter do form a kind of emotional currency in Juno's home environment, Juno uses them to make herself cool and aloof, in the way teenagers like to give themselves status. It is also the quality about her that makes Mark start to fall in love with her, exposing his relationship with Vanessa as very weak.

Juno's External Wound, her major problem in the story, is being pregnant at sixteen, going through a painful process of being seen as different to her peers, giving birth, and giving up her child. Her External Gift is love with Paulie Bleeker. He is her Gift because he is the right guy for her. He is nice, caring, and supportive. For instance, he is the only person at school who doesn't make her feel fat and ugly. He is always pleased to see her and desperate for the relationship.

Juno eventually has to sacrifice her Internal Gift so that she can regain closeness with Paulie after she has pushed him away. Being the right guy for her, who adores her and never wanted to be pushed away, he can't deal with her defensive mixed messages. He is a slightly hapless sixteen-year-old, who has never coped with anything as major as being a father, but only wants to do his best as he feels equally responsible. As Juno rejects him, he feels he has to back off if that is what she really wants. This is what her defensive big mouth seems to be implying! Juno has to learn that being emotionally open is the only way to be reunited with Paulie.

Juno's Internal Wound, her loss of her mother, is healed by Juno becoming a mother herself and giving up her child to a better family, to Vanessa, who will be a single mom. Just like Juno's own mother gave her up by leaving her with the better "real" family of her father and stepmom, Juno is going to do the same thing with her child. Although at the beginning Juno wanted to give her child parents who will never break up, she has to learn that this is a childlike fantasy. By repeating her mother's abandonment in another form, Juno learns that abandonment can lead to a happy family after all. This heals her Internal Wound *and* heals the Metaphoric Wound of the story.

PHASES

Identity Phases

By getting pregnant, the Transition phase runs all the way through Juno's story. Everything changes as fast as Juno's body does: her family's priorities in helping her, school friends' attitudes to her, feelings toward Paulie, and feelings toward herself. Being so young, Juno is not psychologically prepared for the Transition. She's on a roller coaster of conscious and unconscious reactions, her own and others, to her changing state, and it is only toward the end of the story she takes control.

Juno's Maternal Lessons are complex and result in Juno feeling more ambivalent about women than men. Maternal Lessons are also an underlying phase throughout the story, because although Juno is consciously doing her best to be the opposite of her mother, she is unconsciously repeating her Maternal Lessons. She wants to be a good mom to her child. Her mother's abandonment has taught her that mothers aren't the best parents. The closest she has to a mother/daughter relationship is with her stepmom. Bren has her own daughter, Juno's half-sister, but she doesn't really differentiate in her attitude between the two girls. She refers to Juno as "my kid." In this way, Juno's attitudes to women are ambivalent. They have taught her that the nonbiological mother can be better than your own. This is why she finally trusts Vanessa as a single mom to adopt her child.

Juno doesn't have much experience with Father Distance as her own father brought her up. Accordingly, she turns to men for love and emotional support. She basically trusts men, because her own father wasn't very distant at all and is a hands-on Nurturer. Her first experience with Father Distance is through Mark, the prospective adopter of Juno's baby. Juno bonds with Mark and seeks him out for support on her own. Having rejected Paulie, she begins to innocently flirt with Mark. When Mark finally tells Juno he's walking out on Vanessa and getting his own flat so they can have a relationship, it destroys Juno's illusion that men are the good guys. Juno realizes that if he can abandon Vanessa, he can abandon the baby. This is her first real experience with Father Distance and male abandonment of the family unit.

Relating Phases

Desire for Union, in the form of losing her virginity with Paulie, is the inciting incident of Juno's story, immediately propelling her on the massive Transition of pregnancy. Juno Self-Relegates when she rejects Paulie. Instead of letting him show her love, she has low self-esteem issues brought on by getting huge, and her unconscious fear of repeating her own mother's patterns. Pregnancy forms a long Retreat for Juno, as she slowly becomes an Outsider in her school life and integrates into the Lorings household by turning to Mark for support. This is her misguided Desire for Union with Mark. Although consciously he is an idealized father for her child, she also wants to appear attractive to him. For instance, she puts on makeup before visiting him. At school, Juno has an Eruption with Paulie when she accuses him of fancying someone else. He angrily counters that he should be angry with her.

After Juno gives birth, she Retreats inwardly. She doesn't want to see the baby, because she and Paulie agree he is Vanessa's. Juno is supported in the painful postnatal state of Transition back to her old self by her father and Paulie, who both give her tender emotional support in the hospital. At the same time, Bren gives Vanessa a Maternal Lesson in the form of moral support and tells her she looks like any other new mum: "scared shitless."

Momentum Phases

When she first discovers she is pregnant, Juno stands at the Crossroads of her future life. If she has the baby, life will change forever. If she has an abortion, it's all over. She eventually chooses a different Path to Potential, adoption. This leads her into the home of the Lorings. When Mark eventually tells Juno he has fallen for her and wants to leave Vanessa, Juno feels slightly violated by the fact that he sees her sexually, despite her own unconscious collusion with this. Juno has to witness the Eruption between Mark and Vanessa when they break up. Juno flees from their home, her illusions in shatters. Later, she sits in the car, at another metaphoric Crossroads, working out a new option. Taking a Path to Potential, she drives back to the Loring's home and leaves Vanessa the note. *I'm in if you're in.* She has healed her negative Maternal Lessons and now realizes a good enough family is the person or the people who remain constant, as Vanessa has for the baby. Juno now takes the Path to Potential by going back to Paulie to express her real feelings for him. Juno feels the Desire for Union by filling his mailbox with Tic-Tacs and finding him in the sports field to open up to him. In front of all their school friends, they kiss and make up. In the final scene, Juno rides her bike on a Path to Potential back to Paulie's house. They are together again, their Desire for Union with one another ultimately fulfilled.

LAYERS OF CONFLICT

Internal

Juno's pregnancy is a catalyst for her to unconsciously resolve her internal wound of abandonment by her mother.

Significant Other

Juno's confused feelings about herself during her pregnancy make her push Paulie away. Their youth makes them unable to cope with the pregnancy as a couple. Eventually Paulie takes another girl to the prom because Juno told him to. He didn't realize she was unconsciously testing him. By failing the test, Juno turns on him and turns to Mark. Her involvement with Mark leads to huge disappointment when Juno discovers he fancies her. He has overidentified with her youthfulness, and it has made him realize how wrong he and Vanessa are. His decision to leave Vanessa causes Juno huge angst.

Family

Juno's main source of family conflict resides with her feelings about her mother. Vanessa and Mark's relationship problems mean they will be unable to ever create a loving family. This hurts Vanessa and Juno for completely different reasons.

Community

The Women's Clinic is an unpleasant and cynical place. Its atmosphere makes Juno unconsciously realize that her baby symbolizes far more to her than she realized. She cannot go through with the abortion. As a teenage mom, the voice of disapproval comes from the ultrasound nurse, who suggests Juno would be an inadequate mother. At school, the staff views her with disapproval as well. Juno becomes an outcast, the larger she gets. Only her true friends stand by her.

Culture

Juno's loving family helps her avoid stigma at home about being pregnant. She otherwise lives in a culture that is disapproving of teenage parents. Juno's sense of responsibility to her unborn child represents an Amazonian defiance of the hypocrisy in society that suggests that teenagers are inadequate parents.

Psychodynamics in Juno's Relationships

Juno has a tendency to project her self-anger as anger. Because she is pushing Paulie away, she projects this as him wanting to take another girl to the prom. Like all people on the receiving end of projection, Paulie is confused by this and eventually explodes.

Juno denies her need to flirt with Mark. She is aggressive toward Brenda when she tells Juno not to go the Loring's home when Vanessa isn't there, saying Brenda doesn't understand friendship. When Mark tells her that he has feeling for her, she is angry with him. These instances reveal Juno's denial of her role in breaking the Lorings up and kill her fantasy projection that they are the happy family she has always wanted.

LAYERS OF UNION

Internal

Juno is a pretty happy teenager, content with life until she gets pregnant. She's confident and assertive, someone who expresses herself just how she wants. She has no major inhibitions or hang-ups.

Significant Other

Juno has intense happiness with Paulie at the beginning of her story, as they take each other's virginity on a chair. She later finds peace and a sense of soul mate with Mark, until she gets to know why he is so fun to be with — he has never grown up! Later, she reunites with Paulie. They've survived a huge test, and it hasn't dented their relationship.

Family

Juno is close to her father, who she adores and turns to for emotional support. Although not so close to Bren, she definitely relies on her as a practical and reliable mother. She lets Bren handle her pregnancy, just like a mother.

Community

Juno is at home in her community of the school, her friends, and her family. She can joke about her pregnancy tests with the local shopkeeper, for instance. Contraception and abortion services are readily accessible. Although she doesn't take advantage of these, she derives some humor from them.

Culture

Juno's culture allows her to be a normal teenager, with a great deal of freedom to do and act as she pleases. She feels equal.

World

When Mark gives Juno a Japanese magazine with a pregnant superhero, it helps Juno see herself positively by having an image from another culture. Juno also tells Mark that her father named her after the "mean" Roman Goddess Juno, giving another mythic dimension to the story.

Filmography

FILMS

(★★ Recommended Viewing)

The Accused (U.S./Canada/1988)★★

Alice Doesn't Live Here Anymore (U.S./1974)

Aliens (U.S., U.K./1986)★★

All About My Mother (Spain, France/1999)★★

A Ma Soeur! (France, Italy/2001)★★

Amelia (U.S., Canada/2009)

An Education (U.K./2009)★★

A Question of Silence (Netherlands/1982)

At Five in the Afternoon (Iran, France/2003)★★

Australia (Australia, U.S./2008)

Avatar (U.S, U.K./2009)★★

Away from Her (Canada/2006)

Babette's Feast (Denmark/1987)

Baby Mama (U.S./2008)

Bagdad Café (West Germany, U.S./1987)

Bend It Like Beckham (U.K., Germany, U.S./2002)

Boys Don't Cry (U.S./1999)★★

The Brave One (U.S., Australia/2007)

Brick Lane (U.K., India/2007)★★

Bride Wars (U.S./2009)

Bridget Jones's Diary (U.K., Ireland, France/2001)★★

Bridget Jones: The Edge of Reason (U.K., France, Germany, Ireland, U.S./2004)

Brief Encounter (U.K./1945)

Bright Star (U.K., Australia, France/2009)

Burn After Reading (U.S., U.K., France/2008)

Calendar Girls (U.K., U.S./2003)★★

Central Station (Brazil, France/1998)★★

Changeling (U.S./2008)

Cheri (U.K., France, Germany/2009)

Chicago (U.S., Germany/2002)

Chloe (U.S., Canada, France/2009)★★

Chocolat (U.K., U.S./2000)★★

The Circle (Iran, Italy, Switzerland, 2000)★★

Citizen Kane (U.S./1941)

Cold Mountain (U.S./2003)★★

Confessions of a Shopaholic (U.S./2009)

Cracks (U.K., Ireland/2009)

Curse of the Golden Flower (Hong Kong, China/2006)★★

The Departed (U.S., Hong Kong/2006)

The Descent (U.K./2005)★★

The Devil Wears Prada (U.S./2006)★★

Down with Love (U.S., Germany/2003)

The Duchess (U.K., Italy, France/2008)

Earth (India, Canada/1998)★★

East Is East (U.K./1999)

The Edge of Love (U.K./2008)

L'enfer (France, Italy, Belgium, Japan/2005)★★

The English Patient (U.S., U.K./1996)★★

Erin Brockovich (U.S./2000)★★

Female Agents (France/2008)★★

Fire (India, Canada/1996)★★

Fly Away Home (U.S./1996)

Freedom Writers (Germany, U.S./2007)★★

Frida (U.S., Canada, Mexico/2002)★★

4 Months, 3 Weeks and 2 Days (Romania/2007)★★

The Girl with the Dragon Tattoo (Sweden, 2009)

Girl, Interrupted (Germany, U.S./1999)

Gone with the Wind (U.S./1939)★★

Gorillas in the Mist: The Story of Dian Fossey (U.S./1988)

Gothika (U.S./2003)★★

The Handmaid's Tale (U.S., Germany/1990)

Heading South (France, Canada/2005)

He's Just Not That Into You (U.S., Germany, the Netherlands/2009)★★

Hideous Kinky (U.K., France/1998)★★

Hilary and Jackie (U.K./1998)

The Holiday (U.S./2006)★★

The Hours (U.S., U.K./2002)★★

Huit Femmes (France, Italy/2002)

I Love You, Man (U.S./2009)

In Her Shoes (U.S., Germany/2005)★★

Intolerable Cruelty (U.S./2003)

Iris (U.K., U.S./2001)

It's Complicated (U.S./2009)

I've Loved You So Long (France, Germany/2008)★★

International Velvet (U.S./1978)

Jackie Brown (U.S./1997)

Jennifer's Body (U.S./2009)

Julie and Julia (U.S./2009)★★

Juno (U.S., Canada/2007)★★

Kill Bill: Vol. 1 (U.S./2003)

Kill Bill: Vol. 2 (U.S./2004)

Lady Vengeance (South Korea/2005)

The Last Mistress (France, Italy/2007)

La Vie en Rose (France, U.K., Czech Republic/2007)★★

Legally Blonde (U.S./2001)★★

Lost in Translation (U.S., Japan/2003)

Mamma Mia! (U.K., U.S., Germany/2008)★★

Maria Full of Grace (Columbia, Ecuador, U.S./2004)★★

Marley and Me (U.S./2008)

Matilda (U.S./1996)

Memoirs of a Geisha (U.S./2005)

Mermaids (U.S./1990)

The Milk of Sorrow (Spain, Peru/2009)★★

Miss Congeniality (U.S., Australia/2000)★★

Mrs. Parker and the Vicious Circle (U.S./1994)

Mona Lisa Smile (U.S./2003)★★

Monster (U.S., Germany/2003)

Monsters vs Aliens (U.S./2009)★★

The Mother (U.K./2003)

Moulin Rouge (Australia, U.S./2001)

My House in Umbria (U.K., Italy/2003)

My Life Without Me (Spain, Canada/2003)★★

My Summer of Love (U.K./2004)★★

The Nanny Diaries (U.S./2007)★★

Nanny McPhee (U.S., U.K., France/2005)★★

National Velvet (U.S./1944)

Nine (U.S., Italy/2009)

North Country (U.S./2005)★★

New Moon (U.S./2009)

The Other Boleyn Girl (U.K, U.S./2008)

Overboard (U.S./1987)

The Painted Veil (China, U.S./2006)★★

Pan's Labyrinth (Spain, Mexico, U.S./2006)★★

The Piano (Australia, New Zealand, France/1993)★★

Pineapple Express (U.S./2008)

Precious (U.S./2009)★★

Pretty Woman (U.S./1990)

Pride and Prejudice (France, U.K./2005)

The Prime of Miss Jean Brodie (U.K./1969)

The Princess and the Frog (U.S./2009)

The Private Lives of Pippa Lee (U.S./2009)★★

The Proposal (U.S./2009)★★

The Queen (U.K., France, Italy/2006)

Rabbit-Proof Fence (Australia/2002)★★

Reds (U.S./1981)★★

Rendition (U.S./2007)

Romance (France/1999)★★

Saint Trinian's (U.K./2007)★★

Secretary (U.S./2002)★★

The Secret Life of Bees (U.S., 2008)★★

Sex and the City: The Movie (U.S./2008)

She, A Chinese (U.K., France, Germany/2009)

SherryBaby (U.S./2006)

Shirley Valentine (U.K., U.S./1989)

Shrek (U.S./2001)

The Silence of the Lambs (U.S./1991)

Silkwood (U.S./1983)

A Single Man (U.S./2009)

Sister Act (U.S./1992)★★

Slumdog Millionaire (U.K./2008)

Some Like It Hot (U.S./1959)

Something's Gotta Give (U.S./2003)★★

Sophie's Choice (U.K., U.S./1982)★★

Stepmom (U.S./1998)★★

Sylvia (U.K./2003)

Tea with Mussolini (Italy, U.K./1999)

There Will Be Blood (U.S./2007)

10 Things I Hate About You (U.S./1999)

Terminator Salvation (U.S., Germany, U.K., Italy/2009)

Thelma and Louise (U.S., France/1991)★★

Thirteen (U.S./2003)

Titanic (U.S./1997)★★

Transamerica (U.S./2005)★★

TranSylvania (France/2006)

The Truth About Cats & Dogs (U.S./1996)

Tumbleweeds (U.S./1999)

Twilight (U.S./2008)★★

Two Days In Paris (France, Germany/2007)

Under the Skin (U.K./1997)

Under the Tuscan Sun (U.S., Italy/2003)

The Upside of Anger (U.S., Germany, U.K./2005)

Vera Drake (U.K., France, New Zealand/2004)★★

Villa Amalia (France, Switzerland/2009)★★

The Virgin Suicides (U.S./1999)

Volver (Spain/2006)★★

Waiting to Exhale (U.S./1995)

Waitress (U.S./2007)★★

Water (Canada, India/2005)★★

Whale Rider (New Zealand, Germany/2002)

What Happens in Vegas (U.S./2008)

What Lies Beneath (U.S./2000)

When Harry Met Sally (U.S./1989)

The Young Victoria (U.K., U.S./2009)

TELEVISION

Army Wives (U.S./2007)

Brothers and Sisters (U.S./2006)

Criminal Minds (U.S./2005)

CSI: Crime Scene Investigation (U.S./2000)

Damages (U.S./2007)

Desperate Housewives (U.S./2004)

Entourage (U.S./2004)

The Gilmour Girls (U.S./2000)

The Good Wife (U.S./2009)

House M.D. (U.S./2004)

Medium (U.S./2005)

Mistresses (U.K./2008)

No Angels (U.K./2004)

Sex and the City (U.S./1998)

Ugly Betty (U.S./2006)

ABOUT THE AUTHOR

HELEN JACEY is a screenwriter, screen-writing teacher, and story consultant.

Prior to screenwriting, Helen spent many years working for international aid agencies to provide psychological support services for women and children. She has also taught creativity and self-development courses to hundreds of women.

Helen graduated with an M.A. in Screenwriting at the London Institute in 2001. She wrote her first screenplay in 1999 and has either sold or op-tioned every screenplay she has written. Helen's interest in the stories of heroines led her to undertake a Ph.D. in Screenwriting at the University of the Arts London.

Her two-day seminar, Helen Jacey's *Writing the Heroine's Story*, has helped many international screenwriters think about the real dif-ferences when the hero is a heroine. She also lectures on screenwriting at many leading universities.

Helen spends her time in the U.K. and Los Angeles.

For further information about screenwriting, training, con-sultancy, lecturing, or *Helen Jacey's Writing the Heroine's Story* seminar, please visit *www.helenjacey.com*

You can contact Helen at: *helenjacey@gmail.com*

THE VIRGIN'S PROMISE
WRITING STORIES OF FEMININE CREATIVE, SPIRITUAL, AND SEXUAL AWAKENING

KIM HUDSON

FOREWORD BY **CHRISTOPHER VOGLER**, AUTHOR OF
THE WRITER'S JOURNEY 3RD EDITION

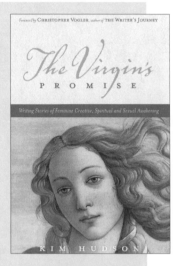

The Virgin's Promise demystifies the complexities of archetypes and clearly outlines the steps of a Virgin's Journey to realize her dream. Audiences need to see more than brave, self-sacrificing Heroes. They need to see Virgins who bring their talents and self-fulfilling joys to life. *The Virgin's Promise* describes this journey with beats that feel incredibly familiar but have not been illustrated in any other screenwriting book. It explores the yin and yang of the Virgin and Hero journeys to take up their power as individuals, and includes a practical guide to putting this new theory into action.

- 13 distinct beats that do for the Virgin what Vogler did for the Hero.

- Easy-to-use tables to demystify the nature of archetypes.

- Filmographies with beat descriptions for 21 Virgin and 10 Hero films including *Ever After*, *Bend It Like Beckham*, *Billy Elliot*, *Brokeback Mountain*, *Wedding Crashers*, *Blood Diamond*, and *The Bourne Identity*.

- Clear explanations of how the Virgin works with the Hero.

"For a work as thought provoking and even profound as this, The Virgin's Promise *is thankfully accessible and not for a minute esoteric during its read. The icing on the cake is Hudson's style and use of language. At once simple and yet complex.* The Virgin's Promise *is a bit like the perfect haiku: Sparse and philosophical"*

> — Deepa Mehta, screenwriter/producer of *Fire, Earth, Water*
> and *Bollywood/Hollywood*

"A story well told can change the world. Hudson unlocks the secret to writing stories of self-fulfillment in this lovely and inspiring book. A must read for all storytellers and screenwriters."

> — Mireille Soria, producer of *Ever After*

KIM HUDSON'S personal journey and scholarly inquiry combined to develop this theory of the Virgin's archetypal structure. Over the past four years Kim has given workshops and classes in the Vancouver area on the Virgin's Promise.

$19.95 · 180 PAGES · ORDER NUMBER 142RLS · ISBN: 9781932907728

24 HOURS | **1.800.833.5738** | **WWW.MWP.COM**

THE WRITER'S JOURNEY - 3RD EDITION
MYTHIC STRUCTURE FOR WRITERS

CHRISTOPHER VOGLER

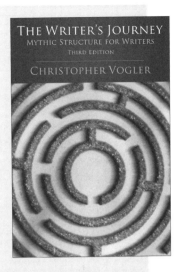

BEST SELLER
OVER 180,000 COPIES SOLD!

See why this book has become an international best seller and a true classic. *The Writer's Journey* explores the powerful relationship between mythology and storytelling in a clear, concise style that's made it required reading for movie executives, screenwriters, playwrights, scholars, and fans of pop culture all over the world.

Both fiction and nonfiction writers will discover a set of useful myth-inspired storytelling paradigms (i.e., "The Hero's Journey") and step-by-step guidelines to plot and character development. Based on the work of Joseph Campbell, *The Writer's Journey* is a must for all writers interested in further developing their craft.

The updated and revised third edition provides new insights and observations from Vogler's ongoing work on mythology's influence on stories, movies, and man himself.

"This book is like having the smartest person in the story meeting come home with you and whisper what to do in your ear as you write a screenplay. Insight for insight, step for step, Chris Vogler takes us through the process of connecting theme to story and making a script come alive."
> – Lynda Obst, Producer, *Sleepless in Seattle, How to Lose a Guy in 10 Days*;
> Author, *Hello, He Lied*

"This is a book about the stories we write, and perhaps more importantly, the stories we live. It is the most influential work I have yet encountered on the art, nature, and the very purpose of storytelling."
> – Bruce Joel Rubin, Screenwriter, *Stuart Little 2, Deep Impact,*
> *Ghost, Jacob's Ladder*

CHRISTOPHER VOGLER is a veteran story consultant for major Hollywood film companies and a respected teacher of filmmakers and writers around the globe. He has influenced the stories of movies from *The Lion King* to *Fight Club* to *The Thin Red Line* and most recently wrote the first installment of *Ravenskull*, a Japanese-style manga or graphic novel. He is the executive producer of the feature film *P.S. Your Cat is Dead* and writer of the animated feature *Jester Till*.

$26.95 · 448 PAGES · ORDER NUMBER 76RLS · ISBN: 9781932907360

SAVE THE CAT!®
THE LAST BOOK ON
SCREENWRITING YOU'LL EVER NEED!

BLAKE SNYDER

He's made millions of dollars selling screenplays to Hollywood and now screenwriter Blake Snyder tells all. "Save the Cat!®" is just one of Snyder's many ironclad rules for making your ideas more marketable and your script more satisfying – and saleable, including:
- The four elements of every winning logline.
- The seven immutable laws of screenplay physics.
- The 10 genres and why they're important to your movie.
- Why your Hero must serve your idea.
- Mastering the Beats.
- Mastering the Board to create the Perfect Beast.
- How to get back on track with ironclad and proven rules for script repair.

This ultimate insider's guide reveals the secrets that none dare admit, told by a show biz veteran who's proven that you can sell your script if you can save the cat.

"Imagine what would happen in a town where more writers approached screenwriting the way Blake suggests? My weekend read would dramatically improve, both in sellable/producible content and in discovering new writers who understand the craft of storytelling and can be hired on assignment for ideas we already have in house."
> – From the Foreword by Sheila Hanahan Taylor, Vice President, Development at Zide/Perry Entertainment, whose films include *American Pie, Cats and Dogs, Final Destination*

"One of the most comprehensive and insightful how-to's out there. Save the Cat!® is a must-read for both the novice and the professional screenwriter."
> – Todd Black, Producer, *The Pursuit of Happyness, The Weather Man, S.W.A.T, Alex and Emma, Antwone Fisher*

"Want to know how to be a successful writer in Hollywood? The answers are here. Blake Snyder has written an insider's book that's informative – and funny, too."
> – David Hoberman, Producer, *The Shaggy Dog* (2005), *Raising Helen, Walking Tall, Bringing Down the House, Monk* (TV)

BLAKE SNYDER, besides selling million-dollar scripts to both Disney and Spielberg, was one of Hollywood's most successful spec screenwriters. Blake's vision continues on *www.blakesnyder.com.*

$19.95 · 216 PAGES · ORDER NUMBER 34RLS · ISBN: 9781932907001

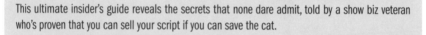

 # THE MYTH OF MWP

In a dark time, a light bringer came along, leading the curious and the frustrated to clarity and empowerment. It took the well-guarded secrets out of the hands of the few and made them available to all. It spread a spirit of openness and creative freedom, and built a storehouse of knowledge dedicated to the betterment of the arts.

The essence of the Michael Wiese Productions (MWP) is empowering people who have the burning desire to express themselves creatively. We help them realize their dreams by putting the tools in their hands. We demystify the sometimes secretive worlds of screenwriting, directing, acting, producing, film financing, and other media crafts.

By doing so, we hope to bring forth a realization of 'conscious media' which we define as being positively charged, emphasizing hope and affirming positive values like trust, cooperation, self-empowerment, freedom, and love. Grounded in the deep roots of myth, it aims to be healing both for those who make the art and those who encounter it. It hopes to be transformative for people, opening doors to new possibilities and pulling back veils to reveal hidden worlds.

MWP has built a storehouse of knowledge unequaled in the world, for no other publisher has so many titles on the media arts. Please visit www.mwp.com where you will find many free resources and a 25% discount on our books. Sign up and become part of the wider creative community!

Onward and upward,

Michael Wiese
Publisher/Filmmaker

FILM & VIDEO BOOKS

SCREENWRITING | WRITING

And the Best Screenplay Goes to... | Dr. Linda Seger | $26.95
Archetypes for Writers | Jennifer Van Bergen | $22.95
Bali Brothers | Lacy Waltzman, Matthew Bishop, Michael Wiese | $12.95
Cinematic Storytelling | Jennifer Van Sijll | $24.95
Could It Be a Movie? | Christina Hamlett | $26.95
Creating Characters | Marisa D'Vari | $26.95
Crime Writer's Reference Guide, The | Martin Roth | $20.95
Deep Cinema | Mary Trainor-Brigham | $19.95
Elephant Bucks | Sheldon Bull | $24.95
Fast, Cheap & Written That Way | John Gaspard | $26.95
Hollywood Standard – 2nd Edition, The | Christopher Riley | $18.95
Horror Screenwriting | Devin Watson | $24.95
I Could've Written a Better Movie than That! | Derek Rydall | $26.95
Inner Drives | Pamela Jaye Smith | $26.95
Moral Premise, The | Stanley D. Williams, Ph.D. | $24.95
Myth and the Movies | Stuart Voytilla | $26.95
Power of the Dark Side, The | Pamela Jaye Smith | $22.95
Psychology for Screenwriters | William Indick, Ph.D. | $26.95
Reflections of the Shadow | Jeffrey Hirschberg | $26.95
Rewrite | Paul Chitlik | $16.95
Romancing the A-List | Christopher Keane | $18.95
Save the Cat! | Blake Snyder | $19.95
Save the Cat! Goes to the Movies | Blake Snyder | $24.95
Screenwriting 101 | Neill D. Hicks | $16.95
Screenwriting for Teens | Christina Hamlett | $18.95
Script-Selling Game, The | Kathie Fong Yoneda | $16.95
Stealing Fire From the Gods, 2nd Edition | James Bonnet | $26.95
Talk the Talk | Penny Penniston | $24.95
Way of Story, The | Catherine Ann Jones | $22.95
What Are You Laughing At? | Brad Schreiber | $19.95
Writer's Journey – 3rd Edition, The | Christopher Vogler | $26.95
Writer's Partner, The | Martin Roth | $24.95
Writing the Action Adventure Film | Neill D. Hicks | $14.95
Writing the Comedy Film | Stuart Voytilla & Scott Petri | $14.95
Writing the Killer Treatment | Michael Halperin | $14.95
Writing the Second Act | Michael Halperin | $19.95
Writing the Thriller Film | Neill D. Hicks | $14.95
Writing the TV Drama Series, 2nd Edition | Pamela Douglas | $26.95
Your Screenplay Sucks! | William M. Akers | $19.95

FILMMAKING

Film School | Richard D. Pepperman | $24.95
Power of Film, The | Howard Suber | $27.95

PITCHING

Perfect Pitch – 2nd Edition, The | Ken Rotcop | $19.95
Selling Your Story in 60 Seconds | Michael Hauge | $12.95

SHORTS

Filmmaking for Teens, 2nd Edition | Troy Lanier & Clay Nichols | $24.95
Making It Big in Shorts | Kim Adelman | $22.95

BUDGET | PRODUCTION MANAGEMENT

Film & Video Budgets, 5th Updated Edition | Deke Simon | $26.95
Film Production Management 101 | Deborah S. Patz | $39.95

DIRECTING | VISUALIZATION

Animation Unleashed | Ellen Besen | $26.95

Cinematography for Directors | Jacqueline Frost | $29.95
Citizen Kane Crash Course in Cinematography | David Worth | $19.95
Directing Actors | Judith Weston | $26.95
Directing Feature Films | Mark Travis | $26.95
Fast, Cheap & Under Control | John Gaspard | $26.95
Film Directing: Cinematic Motion, 2nd Edition | Steven D. Katz | $27.95
Film Directing: Shot by Shot | Steven D. Katz | $27.95
Film Director's Intuition, The | Judith Weston | $26.95
First Time Director | Gil Bettman | $27.95
From Word to Image, 2nd Edition | Marcie Begleiter | $26.95
I'll Be in My Trailer! | John Badham & Craig Modderno | $26.95
Master Shots | Christopher Kenworthy | $24.95
Setting Up Your Scenes | Richard D. Pepperman | $24.95
Setting Up Your Shots, 2nd Edition | Jeremy Vineyard | $22.95
Working Director, The | Charles Wilkinson | $22.95

DIGITAL | DOCUMENTARY | SPECIAL

Digital Filmmaking 101, 2nd Edition | Dale Newton & John Gaspard | $26.95
Digital Moviemaking 3.0 | Scott Billups | $24.95
Digital Video Secrets | Tony Levelle | $26.95
Greenscreen Made Easy | Jeremy Hanke & Michele Yamazaki | $19.95
Producing with Passion | Dorothy Fadiman & Tony Levelle | $22.95
Special Effects | Michael Slone | $31.95

EDITING

Cut by Cut | Gael Chandler | $35.95
Cut to the Chase | Bobbie O'Steen | $24.95
Eye is Quicker, The | Richard D. Pepperman | $27.95
Film Editing | Gael Chandler | $34.95
Invisible Cut, The | Bobbie O'Steen | $28.95

SOUND | DVD | CAREER

Complete DVD Book, The | Chris Gore & Paul J. Salamoff | $26.95
Costume Design 101, 2nd Edition | Richard La Motte | $24.95
Hitting Your Mark, 2nd Edition | Steve Carlson | $22.95
Sound Design | David Sonnenschein | $19.95
Sound Effects Bible, The | Ric Viers | $26.95
Storyboarding 101 | James Fraioli | $19.95
There's No Business Like Soul Business | Derek Rydall | $22.95
You Can Act! | D.W. Brown | $24.95

FINANCE | MARKETING | FUNDING

Art of Film Funding, The | Carole Lee Dean | $26.95
Bankroll | Tom Malloy | $26.95
Complete Independent Movie Marketing Handbook, The | Mark Steven Bosko | $39.95
Getting the Money | Jeremy Jusso | $26.95
Independent Film and Videomakers Guide – 2nd Edition, The | Michael Wiese | $29.95
Independent Film Distribution | Phil Hall | $26.95
Shaking the Money Tree, 3rd Edition | Morrie Warshawski | $26.95

MEDITATION | ART

Mandalas of Bali | Dewa Nyoman Batuan | $39.95

OUR FILMS

Dolphin Adventures: DVD | Michael Wiese and Hardy Jones | $24.95
Hardware Wars: DVD | Written and Directed by Ernie Fosselius | $14.95
On the Edge of a Dream | Michael Wiese | $16.95
Sacred Sites of the Dalai Lamas– DVD, The | Documentary by Michael Wiese | $24.95